Common Mistakes in English

Published by :
Lotus Press Publishers & Distributors

Common Mistakes in English

Surya Kumar

4735/22, Prakash Deep Building
Ansari Road, Darya Ganj,
New Delhi - 110002

Lotus Press : Publishers & Distributors
Unit No. 220, 2nd Floor, 4735/22, Prakash Deep Building,
Ansari Road, Darya Ganj, New Delhi- 110002
Ph.: 98118-38000
• E-mail : lotuspress1984@gmail.com
www.lotuspress.co.in

Common Mistakes in English

ISBN: 81-8382-181-2

Printed & Published by : **Lotus Press Publisher & Distributors,** New Delhi-02

PREFACE

The main aim of this book is to enable the students to write, understand and express their views and ideas correctly in English.

It goes without saying that this is the main principal of this book. From beginning to the end, this aim has been kept in view.

The first part of the book includes grammatical rules that every English speaker should know. All the topics have been explained and illustrated simply so that the readers can understand them with their personal efforts.

The guidance of the teacher will help them to grasp these even more easily.

The next part of the book contains spelling mistakes and commonly confused words that would help the reader add accuracy in his or her use of the language.

Special attention has been paid to each and every topic. The salient feature of the book is that a definite plan has been followed in it.

A large number of examples have been given to enable the readers improve their conversation. Special efforts have been made to the book more understandable and useful.

Author

CONTENTS

CHAPTER 1

Parts of Speech

Before correcting the errors and mistakes commonly made by students for whom English is a second language, it is important that they get a clear idea of what is required for writing and speaking grammatically correct English.

For this purpose, it is important that they have a clear understanding of English language.

Let's start with parts of speech.

Parts of Speech

The parts of speech explain the ways that words can be used in various contexts. Every word in English functions as at least one part of speech. Each **part of speech** explains not what the word *is*, but how the word *is used*. In fact, the same word can be a noun in one sentence and a verb or adjective in another sentence.

Traditional grammar classifies words based on eight **parts of speech**: the verb, the noun, the pronoun, the adjective, the adverb, the preposition, the conjunction, and the interjection.

Noun- A word or phrase that names a person, place, thing, quality, or act.

Pronoun- A word that substitutes for a noun and refers to a person, place, thing, idea, or act that was mentioned previously.

Verb - A word or phrase that expresses action, existence, or occurrence.

Adverb- A word that modifies a verb, or an adjective.

Adjective- A word or combination of words that modifies a noun.

Preposition- A word or phrase that shows the relationship of a noun to another noun.

Interjection- A word, phrase, or sound used as an exclamation and capable of standing by itself.

Conjunction - A word that connects other words, phrases, or sentences.

CHAPTER 2

Noun

Definition

A **noun** is the name of a person, place, thing, or idea. It is a word which is used to name a person, animal, place, thing, or an abstract idea.

Examples:

- The **inspector** looked at all the passengers' passes. (person)
- **New Delhi** is the capital of **India**. (place)
- He is writing with a **pen**. (thing)

Types of Nouns

There are different types of nouns. These nouns are used in different conditions to denote different things.

Proper Noun

A **proper noun** is a noun which names a specific person, place, or thing and is always capitalized. The names of days of the week, months, historical documents, institutions, organisations, religions, their holy texts are proper nouns. A proper noun is the opposite of a common noun.

In each of the following sentences, proper nouns are **highlighted**:

- We will see a movie on **Monday**.
- **Taj Mahal** is a well known wonder of the world.
- **Guru Granth Sahib** is a holy book of **Sikhs**.
- **UNICEF** is a very big organization.
- **AIMS** is known as the best institute of medical sciences.

Common Nouns

A common noun is a noun referring to a person, place, or thing in a general sense. We write it with a capital letter only when it begins a sentence. A common noun is the opposite of a proper noun.

In each of the following sentences, common nouns are **highlighted**:

- According to the **villagers**, the nearest **town** is 20 **miles** away.
- All the **gardens** in the **neighbourhood** are full of **roses**.
- **Child labour** should be banned.

Abstract Nouns

An **abstract noun** is a noun which names anything which you can *not* perceive through your five physical senses. The **highlighted** words in the following sentences are all abstract nouns:

In each of the following sentences, abstract nouns are **highlighted**:

- Buying the fire extinguisher was an **afterthought**.
- **Justice** often seems to slip out of our grasp.
- Some scientists believe that **schizophrenia** is transmitted genetically

Countable Nouns

A **countable noun** (or **count noun**) is a noun which names anything or anyone that we can count. It can be singular or plural. Countable nouns are the opposite of non-countable nouns and collective nouns.

In each of the following sentences, **highlighted** words are countable nouns:

- We painted the **table** red and the **chairs** blue.
- John spends every **weekend** with his **books**.
- He found six **dollars** on the road.

Non-Countable Nouns

A **non-countable noun** (or **mass noun**) is a noun which does not have a plural form, and which refers to something that we cannot count. Non-countable nouns are similar to collective nouns, and are the opposite of countable nouns.

The **highlighted** words in the following sentences are non-countable nouns:

- **Oxygen** is essential to human life.
- The **furniture** is heaped in the middle of the room.
- This **water** is very pure.

Collective Nouns

A **collective noun** is a noun naming a group of things, animals, or persons. We can count the individual members of the group, but we usually think of the group as a whole. A collective noun is similar to a non-countable noun, and is the opposite of a countable noun.

In each of the following sentences, **highlighted** word is a collective noun:

- A **bunch** of keys is under the table.
- The **committee** has submitted its report.
- **Public** is required to have patience.

CHAPTER 3

Pronoun

Definition

A pronoun is a word that substitutes for a noun and refers to a person, place, thing, idea, or act that was mentioned previously. It can be secondary in the sentence like *he, she, it, that.* A **pronoun** can replace a noun.

Generally, pronoun stands for (*pro* + noun) or refers to a noun, an individual or individuals or thing or things whose identity is made clear earlier in the text.

For example:

- Give the list to **me.**
- The smallest gift is **mine.**
- **That** is a red ball, but **I** want the yellow ball.
- **What** did **she** say?
- **We** expect from **you** to behave sincerely.

Types of Pronouns

Personal Pronouns

A **personal pronoun** refers to a specific person or thing and changes its form to indicate person, number, gender, and case.

Subjective Personal Pronouns

A **subjective personal pronoun** indicates that the pronoun is acting as the subject of the sentence. The subjective personal pronouns are 'I', 'You', 'She', 'He', 'It', 'We', 'You' and 'They.'

Objective Personal Pronouns

An **objective personal pronoun** indicates that the pronoun is acting as an object of a verb, compound verb, preposition, or infinitive phrase. The objective personal pronouns are: 'Me', 'You', 'Her', 'Him', 'It', 'Us', 'You' and 'Them.'

Possessive Personal Pronouns

A **possessive pronoun** indicates that the pronoun is acting as a marker of possession and defines who owns a particular object or person. The **possessive personal pronouns** are 'Mine', 'Yours', 'Hers', 'His', 'Its', 'Ours' and 'Theirs.'

	Subjective Case		Objective Case		Possessive Case	
Persons	Singular	Plural	Singular	Plural	Singular	Plural
First Person	I	We	Me	Us	My or Mine	Our or Ours
Second Person	Thou, You	You	Thee, You	You	Thy, thine, Your, Yours	Your or Yours
Third Person	He, She, It	They	Him, Her It	Them	His, Her, Its	Their or Theirs

Note: Thou, Thy, Thee, Thine are now seldom used, except when addressing God or in poetry.

'You' and 'Your' are used while speaking to one person or more than one person.

Demonstrative Pronouns

A **demonstrative pronoun** identifies a noun or a pronoun. 'This' and 'These' refer to things that are nearby either in space or in time, while 'That' and 'Those' refer to things that are farther away in space or time.

Demonstrative pronouns are 'This', 'That', 'These', and 'Those.' 'This' and 'That' are used to refer singular nouns or and 'These' and 'Those' are used to refer plural nouns. The family of demonstratives (this/that/these/those/such) can behave either as pronouns or as determiners.

In the following sentences, each of the **highlighted** word is a demonstrative pronoun:

- **These** cookies are delicious.
- **This** book is well written.
- You're going to wear **these**?
- **That** is my book.

Interrogative Pronouns

An **interrogative pronoun** is used to ask questions. The interrogative pronouns are 'Who', 'Whom', 'Which', 'What' and the compounds formed with the suffix 'Ever', as in 'Whoever', 'Whomever', 'Whichever', and 'Whatever'.

Note that either 'Which' or 'What' can also be used as an interrogative adjective, and that 'Who', 'Whom', or 'Which' can also be used as a relative pronoun.

You will find 'Who', 'Whom' and occasionally 'Which' used to refer people, and 'Which' and 'What' used to refer things and to animals.

'Who' acts as the subject of a verb, while 'Whom' acts as the object of a verb.

The **highlighted** word in each of the following sentences is an interrogative pronoun:

- **Which** wants to see the dentist first?
- **Who** wrote this letter?
- **Whom** do you think we should invite?
- To **whom** you want to speak?
- **What** did she say?

Relative Pronouns

A **Relative pronoun** is used to link one phrase or clause to another phrase or clause. The relative pronouns are 'Who', 'Whom', 'That', and 'Which.' The compounds 'Whoever', 'Whomever', and 'Whichever' are also relative pronouns.

You can use the relative pronouns 'Who' and 'Whoever' to refer the subject of a clause or sentence, and 'Whom' and 'Whomever' to refer the objects of a verb, a verbal or a preposition.

In each of the following sentences, the **highlighted** word is a relative pronoun:

- You may invite **whomever** you like to the party.
- **Whoever** broke the window will have to replace it.
- I will read **whichever** manuscript arrives first.
- He seemed to say **whatever** came to mind.
- She will tell you **what** you need to know.

Indefinite Pronouns

An **indefinite pronoun** is a pronoun referring to an identifiable but not specified person or thing. An indefinite pronoun conveys the idea of all, any, none, or some.

The most common indefinite pronouns are 'All', 'Another', 'Any', 'Anybody', 'Anyone', 'Anything', 'Each', 'Everybody', 'Everyone', 'Everything', 'Few', 'Many', 'Nobody', 'None', 'One', 'Several', 'Some', 'Somebody', and 'Someone.'

The **highlighted** words in the following sentences are indefinite pronouns:

- **Many** were called for interview, but only twelve turned up.
- **Everything** was thrown onto the floor.
- Make sure you give **everyone** a copy of the notes.

Reflexive Pronouns

A **Reflexive pronoun** is used to refer back to the subject of the clause or sentence.The reflexive pronouns are 'Myself', 'Yourself', 'Herself', 'Himself', 'Itself', 'Ourselves', 'Yourselves', and 'Themselves.'

Each of the **highlighted** words in the following sentences is a reflexive pronoun:

- Diabetics give **themselves** insulin shots several times a day.
- After the meeting, I asked **myself** why I am working here.
- Rome usually remembered to send a copy of his e-mail to **himself**.
- We ended up doing the work **ourselves**.

Intensive Pronouns

The intensive pronouns such as myself, yourself, herself, ourselves, themselves, consist of a personal pronoun plus *self* or *selves* and emphasize a noun.

The **highlighted** words in the following sentences are intensive pronouns:

- I **myself** don't know the answer.
- The Prime Minister **himself** said that he would lower taxes.
- They **themselves** promised to come to the party, even though they had an exam on that day.

CHAPTER 4

Verb

Definition

A word or phrase that expresses action, existence, or occurrence is known as a verb. A ***verb*** is often defined as ***a word which shows action or state of being***. The ***verb*** is the heart of a sentence – every sentence must have a ***verb***.

One of the most important thing about ***verbs*** is their relationship to time.

Verbs tell if something has already happened, if it will happen later, or if it is happening now. The verb is the most important step in understanding the meaning of the sentence. In each of the following sentences, the **highlighted** word is a verb:

- The dog **bit** the man.
- The man is **sitting** on the chair and **reading** a book.
- Dracula **bites** his victims on the neck.
- In October, I **will plant** twenty tulip flowers.
- My first teacher **was** Miss Surekha.

Types of Verbs

Intransitive Verb

Intransitive verbs are verbs that express action but do not take an object. The subject and verb express a complete thought without an object. The verb can, however, be followed by an adverb or other modifier.

Examples:

- I **ran**.
- I **ran** swiftly.
- I **ran** in the race.

Transitive Verb

Transitive verbs are verbs that express action that terminates in, or is received by, an object. The object of a transitive verb can be a noun, pronoun, or a noun clause or phrase.

Examples:

- I **threw** the ball. (Noun as object)
- We **beat** them. (Pronoun as object)
- I **think** that you are correct. (Noun clause as object)

Linking Verb

Linking verbs are verbs of the senses like 'feel', 'look', 'smell', or 'taste', and a limited number of other verbs like 'be', 'seem', 'become', or 'remain' that link the subject of the sentence with a complement. Linking verbs are always followed by an adjective, noun, or noun phrase that acts as a complement.

Examples:

- He **is** a lawyer. (Noun as complement)
- I **feel** tired. (Adjective as complement)

- It **seems** that we will lose the game. (Noun clause as complement)

Passive-voice Verb

Passive-voice verbs are verbs that allow the subject to receive the action rather than to do the action. Passive-voice verbs are made by using some form of the verb 'be' that is followed by a verb ending in -en or -ed. Only transitive verbs can be turned into the passive form.

Examples:

- Our team was **beaten** at softball. ('By the opposing team' is implied.)
- The building was **destroyed** by the wrecking crew.
- The ball was **thrown** by me.

Chapter 5

Adverb

Definition

An **adverb** can modify a verb, an adjective, another adverb, a phrase, or a clause. An adverb indicates manner, time, place, cause, or degree and answers questions such as 'how', 'when', 'where', 'how much', etc.

While some adverbs can be identified by their characteristic 'ly' suffix, most of them must be identified by the grammatical relationships within the sentence or clause as a whole. An adverb can be found in various places within the sentence.

In the following examples, each of the **highlighted** words is an adverb:

- The washerman **quickly** washed the clothes.
- The man waited **patiently** for a doctor.
- Rahul can speak anything **boldly.**
- **Unfortunately**, the bank closed at three today.
- Sita can walk **elegantly**.

Types of Adverbs

Conjunctive Adverbs

Conjunctive adverb is used to join two clauses together. Some of the most common conjunctive adverbs are 'also', 'consequently', 'finally', 'furthermore', 'hence', 'however', 'incidentally', 'indeed', 'instead', 'likewise', 'meanwhile', 'nevertheless', 'next', 'nonetheless', 'otherwise', 'still', 'then', 'therefore', and 'thus.'

The **highlighted** words in the following sentences are conjunctive adverbs:

- The government has cut university budgets; **consequently**, class sizes have been increased.
- He did not have all the ingredients the recipe called for; **therefore**, he decided to make something else.
- The crowd waited patiently for three hours; **finally**, the doors to the stadium were opened.
- Batman searched the building; **indeed**, Joker had escaped through a secret door in the basement.

Relative Adverbs

Sometimes when adjectival clause are introduced by what, where, when and why are called the **relative adverbs**: *where, when,* and *why.* Although the entire clause is adjectival and will modify a noun, the relative word itself fulfills an adverbial function.

1. The relative adverb ***where*** will begin a clause that modifies a noun of place:

   My entire family now worships in the <u>church</u> **where** my great grandfather used to be a minister.

2. The ***when*** clause will modify nouns of time:

My favourite month is <u>February</u>, **when** we celebrate Valentine's Day and President's Day.

3. The ***why*** clause will modify the noun ***reason:***

   Do you know the <u>reason</u> **why** John isn't in the class today?

Viewpoint, Focus, and Negative Adverbs

A **viewpoint adverb** generally comes after a noun and is related to an adjective that precedes that noun:

- A successful athletic team is often a good team <u>scholastically</u>.
- Investing all the money in mobiles was probably not a sound idea <u>financially</u>.

A **focus adverb** indicates that what is being communicated is limited to the part that is focused; a focus adverb will tend either to <u>limit</u> the sense of the sentence.

- He got an A grade <u>just</u> for attending the class.

Negative adverb creates a negative meaning in a sentence *without* the use of the usual no/not/neither/nor/never constructions:

- He <u>seldom</u> visits.
- She <u>hardly</u> eats anything since the accident.
- After her long and tedious lectures, <u>rarely</u> was anyone awake.

Kinds of Adverbs

Adverbs of Manner

She moved **slowly** and spoke **quietly**.

Adverbs of Place

She has lived on the island all her life. She still lives **there** now.

Adverbs of Frequency

She takes the boat to the mainland **every day**.

She **often** goes by herself.

Adverbs of Time

She tries to get back **before dark.**

It's starting to get dark **now**.

She finished her tea **first**.

She left **early**.

Adverbs of Purpose

She drives her boat **slowly to avoid hitting** the rocks.

She shops in several stores **to get the best buys**.

Chapter 6

Adjective

Definition

An **adjective** modifies a noun or a pronoun by describing, identifying, or quantifying words. An adjective usually precedes the noun or the pronoun which it modifies.

In the following examples, the **highlighted** words are adjectives:

- The **truck-shaped** balloon floated over the treetops.
- The **small** boat foundered on the **dark** sea.
- The **coal** mines are **dark**.
- **Many** stores have already begun to play **Christmas** music.
- The back room was filled with **large, yellow** rain boots.

Types of Adjectives

Possessive Adjectives

A **possessive adjective** ('my', 'your', 'his', 'her', 'its', 'our', 'their') is similar or identical to a possessive pronoun; however, it is used as an adjective and modifies a noun or a noun phrase.

In the following examples, the **highlighted** words are possessive adjectives:

- I can't complete **my** assignment because I don't have the textbook.
- What is **your** phone number?
- The bakery sold **his** favourite type of bread.
- After many years, she returned to **her** homeland.
- We have lost **our** way in this wood.

Demonstrative Adjectives

The **demonstrative adjectives** 'this', 'these', 'that', 'those', and 'what' are identical to the demonstrative pronouns, but are used as adjectives to modify nouns or noun phrases

In the following examples, the **highlighted** words are possessive adjectives:

- When the librarian tripped over **that** cord, she dropped a pile of books.
- **This** apartment needs to be fumigated.
- Even though my friend preferred **those** plates, I bought these.

Interrogative Adjectives

An **interrogative adjective** ('which' or 'what') is like an interrogative pronoun, except that it modifies a noun or noun phrase rather than standing on its own.

- **Which** plants should be watered twice a week?
- **What** book are you reading?

Indefinite Adjectives

An **indefinite adjective** is similar to an indefinite pronoun, except that it modifies a noun, pronoun, or noun phrase, as in the following sentences:

- **Many people** believe that corporations are under-taxed.
- I will send you **any mail** that arrives after you have moved to Sudbury.
- They found a **few goldfish** floating belly up in the swan pound.

Adjectives are divided into categories as a way of understanding their purpose.

1. **Descriptive Adjective:** These types of adjectives add detail or description to the noun.

In the following examples, the adjective is **bold** and the noun is underlined.

- The **tall** man thought he could reach the **top** shelf of the bookcase.
- After the **difficult** surgery, the **famous** doctors took a nap.
- A **worthwhile** investment had been born.
- Monica said, 'Wow, this is a **great** game.'

2. **Limiting Adjective:** These types of adjectives specify or limit the noun.

In the following examples, the adjective is **bold** and the noun is underlined.

- The **two** teams have met every season since 1932.
- Will you be sitting at the **captain's** table this evening?
- This season, the two are meeting on a **home-and-home** basis, unusual for non-conference rivals.

3. **Predicate Adjective:** This is a special type of adjective that follows a linking verb and modifies (directly refers to) the subject of the sentence.

In the following examples, the predicate adjective is **bold** and the subject/noun is underlined.

- People are **interested** in this game.
- Watching the championship was **fun**.
- If you're not **careful**, the whole group is going to judge you on what you do on this day.
- The two teams look very **similar** in the tempo that they play.
- Stan does not seem **scared** of them.

4. **Verbals as Adjectives:** Two types of verbals can acts as adjectives. Participles are always adjectives and may end in en, ed or ing. Infinitives (to+verb) may act as adjectives, adverbs or nouns.

In the following examples, the verbal is **bold** and the noun it modifies is underlined.

- **Playing** tough defense, both teams push the ball up the floor and score a lot of points.
- It will be an interesting game **to watch**.

5. **Degrees Of Adjectives:**

Adjectives are used to indicate levels, degrees of intensity or comparison

high ____ *base*

higher ____ *comparative*

highest ____ *superlative*

When comparing two things always use the comparative. For example in a comparison between two people the correct usage would be: Bill is taller. Bill is the tallest would require that there be more than two people.

The Basic Types of Adjectives

- **Opinion:** An **opinion** adjective explains what you think about something (other people may not agree with you).

  Examples: *silly, beautiful, horrible, difficult*

- **Size:** A **size** adjective, of course, tells you how big or small something is.

  Examples: *large, tiny, enormous, little*

- **Age:** An **age** adjective tells you how young or old something or someone is.

  Examples: *ancient, new, young, old*

- **Shape:** A **shape** adjective describes the shape of something.

  Examples: *square, round, flat, rectangular*

- **Colour:** A **colour** adjective, of course, describes the colour of something.

  Examples: *blue, pink, reddish, grey*

- **Origin:** An **origin** adjective describes where something comes from.

  Examples: *French, lunar, American, eastern, Greek*

- **Material:** A **material** adjective describes what something is made from.

  Examples: *wooden, metal, cotton, paper*

- **Purpose:** A **purpose** adjective describes what something is used for. These adjectives often end with '-ing'.

  Examples: *sleeping (as in 'sleeping bag'), roasting (as in 'roasting tin')*

CHAPTER 7

Preposition

Definition

A **preposition** links nouns, pronouns and phrases to other words in a sentence. The word or phrase that the preposition introduces is called the object of the preposition.

A preposition usually indicates the temporal, spatial or logical relationship of its object to the rest of the sentence as in the following examples:

- The book is **on** the table.
- The book is **beneath** the table.
- The book is leaning **against** the table.
- The book is **beside** the table.
- She held the book **over** the table.
- She read the book **during** class.

Basic Uses of Prepositions

A preposition shows a relationship between its object and other words in a sentence. The preposition may be in the form of one word (at, by, in, on, etc.) or in the form of a phrase that functions as a unit (in front of, by way of, etc.)

Some of the relationships that prepositions express are place or position, time, manner, direction, and agent.

The book is **on** the desk.	(place or position)
The boy ran **toward** the house.	(direction)
The man arrived **at** ten o'clock.	(time)
He travels **by** train.	(manner)
The book was written **by** him.	(agent)

A preposition + an object forms a phrase. This kind of phrase usually functions as a modifier (adjective or adverb).

The report **of** the meeting was read.	(adjective)
We go to class **at** ten o'clock.	(adverb)

Prepositions of Place or Position

The following sentences show some of the relationship of place or position expressed by various prepositions:

	on	
	in	
	by	
The paper is	beside	the desk.
	near	
	against	
	under	

	behind	
	in back of	
	in front of	

He is sitting	beside near by	her.

Jack is	in inside outside in front of in back of behind underneath on top of	the car.

They walked	across the park. around the park. under the bridge. down the street. up the street. over the hill. through the park. on the sidewalk.

Compare in—on, on—at, at—in in the situations described below:

1. IN—ON

   In general, **in** means beneath the surface; **on** means touching the **surface**.

   - There is a grease spot **on** my coat and a moth hole **in** my sweater.

- We had to drive a large nail **in** the ceiling in order to hang the picture on this wall.

2. ON—AT

   In an address, **on** is used with the name of the street; **at**, with the **house number** and the name of the street.

- He lives **on** Green Street.
- He lives **at** 1236 Green Street.

3. AT—IN

   In referring to location, **at** ordinarily indicates a specified location; **in**, a location within a house, building, city, and so forth.

- I'll meet you **at** the library.
- I'll meet you **at** the information desk in the lobby of the hotel.
- She is **in** the kitchen preparing dinner.

In is also used in referring to a location within a country.

- They own a house **in** Sweden.
- He is **in** Peru, South America, now.

In is ordinarily used in referring to cities.

- He lives **in** Hartford, Connecticut.
- They will arrive **in** Bangkok next month.

At is sometimes used in referring to the arrival of a train, and so forth.

- The train will arrive **at** Philadelphia at 8:10 p.m.

Prepositions of Direction

The prepositions listed in this section are those usually thought of as indicating direction.

However, there is some overlapping of place and direction in such prepositions as from, to, through, up, down, over, under, etc.

The following sentence shows some of the relationships of direction expressed by various prepositions:

	into	
The dog ran	out of	the building.
	toward	

Below is a list of some prepositions that indicate relationships of direction:

1. into — I walked **into** the room and sat down by the fireplace.
2. out of — They ran **out of** the burning building.
3. toward — He walked **toward** the City Hall.
4. by way of — You can go **by way of** the Panama Canal.

Compare in—into in the following situations:

In ordinarily refers to place or position.

- He is **in** his office now.

Into ordinarily refers to motion or action, although **in** is often used interchangeably with **into** in situations of this kind.

Prepositions of Time

The following sentence shows some of the relationships of time expressed by various prepositions:

	at	
	by	
Please arrive	before	10 o'clock.
	after	

Below is a list of some prepositions that indicate relationships of time:

1. at	The baseball game will start **at** 2:30 p.m.
	This gate opens **at** noon and closes **at** midnignt.
by	Try to be there **by** 2 o'clock.
2. in	The train will arrive **in** an hour.
	I must leave **in** a few minutes.
	He goes to work early **in** the morning.
on	Ray's birthday is **on** November 18.
3. for	They stayed **for** three weeks.
during	We saw them often **during** the summer.
since	We have been here **since** 1955.
4. after	Call me again **after** 10 o'clock.
before	He always gets home **before** 6 o'clock
5. until	Why don't you stay **until (till)** Sunday?
(till)	I'll be here **till (until)** 5 o'clock.
6. at the beginning of	I'll call you **at the beginning of** the week.
at the end of	You will receive your check **at the end of** the month.
in the middle of	Let's have lunch sometime **in the middle of** the week.

Compare on—in and for—during—since in the situations described here.

1. ON—IN

   In giving dates, **on** is used before days of the week or before months and day of the month; **in**, before months not followed by the day and before numbers indicating the year.

- **On** Saturday they left for Europe. They took a trip **in** June.
- The store opened **on** May 23, 1950. They moved to Boston **in** July, 1955.
- **On** May 10th they left for Europe. They took a trip to Japan **in** 1954.

2. FOR—DURING—SINCE

   In expressions of time, **for** refers to a period of time, frequently stated in terms of the number of hours, days, weeks, and so forth, and in such expressions as **for a long (short) time, for several** (a few) **minutes, for a little while**, and so forth.

Prepositions of Manner

1. by - You can go **by** bus (car, train, ship, plane, foot).
2. on - I like to travel **on** train (ship, plane).
3. in - We came here **in** a car (taxi).
4. with- I accept your invitation **with** pleasure.
5. like – He walks **like** an old man.

Some Other Types of Prepositions

1. Agent (or Instrument)—by and with
   - This poem was written **by** Walt Whitman.
   - The door is opened **by** a mechanical device.
   - Try opening the door **with** this key.
   - I can write better **with** my own pen.
2. Accompaniment—with
   - He went **with** her to the store.
   - Try some of sauce **with** your meat.

3. Purpose—for
   - This door is **for** emergency exit only.
   - I need to go to the store **for** a loaf of bread.
4. Association—of
   - The new wing **of** the building is almost complete.
   - We heard the news **of** your promotion from Birendra.
5. Measure—of and by
   - I want three quarts **of** milk and a pound of cheese.
   - One-third **of** the students are from South America.
6. Similarity—like
   - This material feels **like** silk.
   - It looks **like** rain.
7. In the Capacity of—as
   - He got a job **as** a project manager..
   - Mr. Khurana will serve **as** the chairman of the committee.

CHAPTER 8

Articles

Definition

An **article** is a word that combines with a noun to indicate the type of reference being made by the noun. The three main articles are *the*, *an* and *a*. An article is sometimes called a *noun marker*, although this is generally considered to be an archaic term. Articles can have various functions:

- A **definite article** is used before singular and plural nouns that refer to a particular member of a group.

  The cat is on the black mat.

- An **indefinite article** is used before singular nouns that refer to any member of a group.

  A cat is a mammal.

Use of articles a, an, the

A, An

- A or An is used for singular. A is used with consonants and An is used with vowels.

He is **an** honest man.

He is **a** smart boy.

- Some words starts with vowel but gives sound of consonant. Like university starts from vowel but gives sound of consonant. He graduated from **a** university. In these cases, we use 'a'.
- Some words starts with consonant but gives sound of vowel. Like honest starts from consonant but gives sound of vowel. She is **an** honest fellow.
- When any adjective is placed before singular noun than we have to use article 'a' and 'an' before that.

  The Ramayana is **an** ancient book of the Hindus.

The

The is used in following conditions.

- With the name of rivers — The Jamuna
- With the name of Countries, Newspapers, Oceans, Mountains, Islands, Community, Religion — The Indian Ocean, The west Indies, The Punjab, The Hindustan Times
- With Sun, Moon and Stars — The Venus
- With superlative degree — the most
- With Adjective — the rich, the poor
- With name of directions — the east

Chapter 9

Interjections

Definition

An **interjection** is a word added to a sentence to convey emotion. It is not grammatically related to any other part of the sentence.

You usually follow an interjection with an exclamation mark. Interjections are uncommon in formal academic prose, except in direct quotations.

The **highlighted** words in the following sentences are interjections:

- **Ouch**, that hurt!
- **Oh no**, I forgot that the exam was today.
- **Hey**! Put that down!
- I heard one guy say to another guy, 'He has a new car, **eh**?'
- I don't know about you but, **good lord**, I think taxes are too high!

Interjections have no real grammatical value, but we use

them quite often, usually more in speaking than in writing. When interjections are inserted into a sentence, they have no grammatical connection to the sentence. An interjection is sometimes followed by an exclamation mark (!) when written.

The table below shows some interjections with examples.

Interjection	**Meaning**	**Example**
Ah	Expressing pleasure	'Ah, that feels good.'
	Expressing realization	'Ah, now I understand.'
	Expressing resignation	'Ah well, it can't be helped.'
	Expressing surprise	'Ah! I've won!'
Alas	Expressing grief or pity	'Alas, she's dead now.'
Dear	Expressing pity	'Oh dear! Does it hurt?'
	Expressing surprise	'Dear me! That's a surprise!'
Eh	Asking for repetition	'It's hot today.' 'Eh?' 'I said it's hot today.'
	Expressing enquiry	'What do you think of that, eh?'
	Expressing surprise	'Eh! Really?'
	Inviting agreement	'Let's go, eh?'
Er	Expressing hesitation	'Lima is the capital of...er...Peru.'
Hello	Expressing greeting	'Hello John. How are you today?'
	Expressing surprise	'Hello! My car's gone!'
Hey	Calling attention	'Hey! Look at that!'
	Expressing surprise, joy etc	'Hey! What a good idea!'
Hi	Expressing greeting	'Hi! What's new?'
Hmm	Expressing hesitation, doubt or disagreement	'Hmm. I'm not so sure.'
oh	Expressing surprise	'Oh! You're here!'
	Expressing pain	'Oh! I've got a toothache.'
	Expressing pleading	'Oh, please say 'yes'!'

Ouch	Expressing pain	'Ouch! That hurts!'
Uh	Expressing hesitation	'Uh...I don't know the answer to that.'
uh-huh	Expressing agreement	'Shall we go?' 'Uh-huh.'
um, umm	Expressing hesitation	'85 divided by 5 is...um...17.'
Well	Expressing surprise	'Well I never!'
	Introducing a remark	'Well, what did he say?'

CHAPTER 10

Conjunction

Definition

A conjunction is a word that connects other words or groups of words. You can use a conjunction to link words, phrases and clauses, as in the following example:

- I ate the pizza **and** the pasta.
- Call the movers **when** you are ready.
- Bob **and** Dan are friends
- It is early **but** we can go.

Coordinating conjunctions are *conjunctions* which connect two equal parts of a sentence. The most common ones are and, or, but, and so which are used in the following ways:

- **and** is used to join or add words together in the sentence – They ate **and** drank.
- **or** is used to show choice or possibilities as in the sentence – He will be here on Monday **or** Tuesday.
- **but** is used to show opposite or conflicting ideas as in the sentence – She is small **but** strong.

- **so** is used to show result as in the sentence – I was tired **so** I went to sleep.

Subordinating conjunctions connect two parts of a sentence that are not equal and will be discussed more in another class. For now, you should know some of the more common *subordinating conjunctions* such as:

- after, before, unless
- although, if, until
- as, since, when
- because, than, while

Correlative conjunctions are pairs of *conjunctions* that work together. In the sentence 'Both Jan and Meg are good swimmers', **both . . .and** are *correlative conjunctions*. The most common *correlative conjunctions* are:

- both . . .and
- either . . . or
- neither . . . nor
- not only . . . but also

Chapter 11

Auxiliary Verbs

The most common auxiliary verbs are 'be,' 'do,' and 'have', and you may also use these verbs on their own. We use 'will' and 'shall' to express future time.

Some Auxiliary Verbs

Can, Could

- Can is used to show the physical ability or work ability of a person.

  He **can** study for a day.
- Could is used as a past tense of can.

  He **could** do this work alone.
- In negative sentences we add not with can or could.

Note that 'cannot' is one word but we write could not as two different words.

We **cannot** stop laughing.

- In interrogative sentences we start the sentence with can or could.
- Don't use is, am, are with can or could.

May, Might

- May is used for taking permissions.

  May I come in sir?
- May is used for desire, possibility, blessing.

  May God give you long time!

  It may rain.
- Might is used as a past tense of may.

  We ran fast so that we **might** catch the bus.

Should, Would

- Would is used as a past tense of will.

  Would you like to have tea?
- Should is used as a past tense of shall. It also used for advice, duty, purpose.

  We **should** obey our elders.
- Always use should with lest.

  Work hard lest you **should** fail.
- Would is used for determination, threat, habit.

  He **would** come to the office on time.

Ought, Must

- Ought and must are used to show the duty

  I **must** reach home by 10 o' clock.
- Always use to with ought.

  You **ought** to help me.
- Ought is used for moral duty.

  We **ought** to look after our aged parents.

Chapter 12

Tenses in English

Definition

A verb form that indicates, or can indicate, a relationship between the time the action in a verb occurs and the time the verb is uttered. A verb tense can also give an indication of the duration of the verb's action and when or if it is completed.

Tenses form the grammatical category of verbs used to express distinctions of time.

The tense of a verb tells us **when** the action was done. The action can be done in the past, present or future.

Past ←	**Present**	→ **Future**
Yesterday I **worked** late	Today I **work** late I **am working** late	Tomorrow **I shall work** late I **am working** late

Active	**Simple**	**Continuous**
Present	I work	I am working
Past	I worked	I was working
Future	I will work	I will be working

Present Perfect	I have worked	I have been working
Past Perfect	I had worked	I had been working
Future Perfect	I will have worked	I will have been working

Importance of Helping Verbs

In English, there are three basic tenses: present, past, and future. Each has a perfect form, indicating completed action; each has a progressive or continuous form, indicating ongoing action; and each has a perfect form indicating action has been done and perfect progressive or continuous form, indicating ongoing action that will be completed at some definite time. Here is a list of examples of these tenses and their definitions:

	Simple Forms	**Progressive Forms**	**Perfect Forms**	**Perfect Progressive Forms**
Present	take/s/do/does	am/is/are taking	have/has taken	have/has been taking
Past	took/did	was/were taking	had taken	had been taking
Future	will/shall take	will be taking	will have taken	will have been taking

CHAPTER 13

The Present Tense

The present tense indicates the running time, or we can say the time of today. Present tense expresses an unchanging, repeated, or reoccurring action or situation that exists only now. It can also represent a widespread truth.

Example	Meaning
The mountains **are** tall and white.	Unchanging action
Every year, the school council **elects** new members.	Recurring action
Pb <u>is</u> the chemical symbol for lead.	Widespread truth

The Simple Present Tense

The simple present tense is the tense used to describe actions that are timeless. If the time of the action can be defined, then the present simple tense is used. The time and/or place is stated or understood.

The Present Simple Tense is used in the following situations:

- permanent actions

- actions that happen on a regular basis
- facts
- statements that are always true
- to state existence
- to state feeling
- static verbs
- general actions

Work	**I / you / we / they**	**he / she / it**
Affirmative	I/you/we/they **work.**	He/she/it **works.**
Negative	I/you/we/they **don't work.**	He/she/it **doesn't work.**
Question	**Do** I/you/we/they **work?**	**Does** he/she/it **work?**
Short answers	**Do** you **work?**	**Does** she work?
	Yes, I **do.**	Yes, she **does.**
	No, I **don't.**	No, she **doesn't.**

The Present Continuous Tense

Use the present continuous form of a verb when:

The action isn't a single action, it is an action that carries on. It is good for describing what people are doing at a particular moment.

Example: I **am kicking** the ball.

He **is walking** the dog.

The present continuous is made by having **am**, **is** or **are** + the **verb's 1st form + 'ing'**

Work	**I**	**he / she / it**	**you / we / they**
Affirmative	I **am** working	He **is** working	They **are** working
Negative	I **am not** working	She **is not** working	We **are not** working
Question	**Am** I working?	**Is** he working?	**Are** you working?

Short answers	**Are** you working?	**Is** she working?	**Are** they working?
	Yes, I **am** working.	Yes, she **is** working.	Yes, they **are** working.
	No, I'**m not** working.	No, she **isn't** working.	No, they **aren't** working.

The Present Perfect Tense

The simple present tense is used to show that present work has completed. This action describes what people have done in particular moment.

The present perfect is made by having **has/have + verb's 3rd form**.

Work	**I**	**he / she / it**	**you / we / they**
Affirmative	I **have** worked	He **has** worked	They **have** worked
Negative	I **haven't** worked	She **has not** worked	We **haven't** worked
Question	**Have** I worked?	**Has** he worked?	**Have** he worked?
Short answers	**Have** you worked?	**Has** he worked?	**Have** they worked?
	Yes, I have worked.	Yes, he **has** worked.	Yes, they **have** worked.
	No, I **haven't** worked.	No, he **hasn't** worked.	No, they **haven't** worked.

The Present Perfect Continuous Tense

The present perfect continuous tense is used to show that work has completed and still going on. This action describes that people are continuously working for many hours and still they continue it.

The present perfect is made by having **has/have + verb's 1st form** + ing.

Work	I	he / she / it	You / we / they
Affirmative	I **have** been working for 2 hours.	He **has** been working for 2 hours.	They **have** been working for 2 hours.
Negative	I **haven't** been working for 2 hours.	She **has not been** working for 2 hours.	We **haven't been** working for 2 hours.
Question	**Have** I been working for 2 hours?	**Has** he been working for 2 hours?	**Have** he been working for 2 hours?
Short answers	**Have** you been working?	**Has** he been working?	**Have** he been working?
	Yes, I have been working.	Yes, he **has** been working.	Yes, they **have** been working.
	No, I **haven't** been working.	No, he **hasn't** been working.	No, they **haven't** been working.

CHAPTER 14

The Past Tense

The past tense indicates the time which has passed. In other words, it is the time of yesterday. Past tense expresses an action or situation that was started and finished in the past. Most past tense verbs end in **-ed**. The irregular verbs have **special past tense forms** which must be memorized.

Example	**Form**
World War II **ended** in 1945.	Regular -ed past
Mr. Bru **wrote** 'The Old Man and the Sea.'	Irregular form

To make the past tense of regular verbs we add 'ed' or 'd'

verb	**past tense**
love	loved
walk	walked
listen	listened

The verb changes in the past tense of irregular verbs

verb	**past tense**
go	went

have	had
make	made

The Simple Past Tense

Use the simple past form of a verb when you are talking about an action that took place at a specific point in the past and that is now finished.

Example: I kick**ed** the ball and scor**ed** a goal.

I walk**ed** the dog yesterday.

I **went** to Florida last year.

Work	**I / you / we / they**	**he / she / it**
Affirmative	I/you/we/they **worked.**	He/she/it **worked.**
Negative	I/you/we/they **didn't work.**	He/she/it **didn't work.**
Question	**Did** I/you/we/they **work?**	**Did** he/she/it **work?**
Short answers	**Did** you **work?**	**Did** she work?
	Yes, I **did.**	Yes, she **did.**
	No, I **did.**	No, she **did.**

The Past Continuous Tense

Use the past continuous form of a verb when you want to talk about a long action that carried on in the past. The continuous past is often used to describe what people were doing when something else happened.

Example: I **was kicking** the ball..

He **was walking**..

The past continuous is made by having **was**, or **were** + the verb + '**ing**'.

Work	**I**	**he / she / it**	**you / we / they**
Affirmative	I **was** working	He **was** working	They **were** working

Negative	I **was not** working	She **was not** working	We **were not** working
Question	**Was** I working?	**Was** he working?	**Were** you working?
Short answers	**Were** you working?	**Was** she working?	**Were** they working?
	Yes, I **was** working.	Yes, she **was** working.	Yes, they **were** working.
	No, I **was not** working.	No, she **wasn't** working.	No, they **weren't** working.

The Past Perfect Tense

The simple past tense is used to show that past work has completed. This action describes what people have done in particular moment. Past perfect tense describes action that took place in the past before another past action.

The past perfect is made by having **had + verb's 3rd form**.

Work	**I**	**He / she / it**	**you / we / they**
Affirmative	I **had** worked	He **had** worked	They **had** worked
Negative	I **hadn't** worked	She **had not** worked	We **hadn't** worked
Question	**Had** I worked?	**Had** he worked?	**Had** he worked?
Short answers	**Had** you worked?	**Has** he worked?	**Have** they worked?
	Yes, I had worked.	Yes, he **had** worked.	Yes, they **had** worked.
	No, I **hadn't** worked.	No, he **hadn't** worked.	No, they **hadn't** worked.

The Past Perfect Continuous Tense

The past perfect continuous tense is used to show that work has completed in past and still going on. This action describes that people are continuously working for many hours and still they continue it.

The past perfect is made by having **has/have + verb's 1st form**+ ing.

Work	I	he / she / it	You / we / they
Affirmative	I **had** been working for 2 hours.	He **had** been working for 2 hours.	They **had** been working for 2 hours.
Negative	I **hadn't** been working for 2 hours.	She **had not been** working for 2 hours.	We **hadn't been** working for 2 hours.
Question	**Had** I been working for 2 hours?	**Had** he been working for 2 hours?	**Had** they been working for 2 hours?
Short answers	**Had** you been working?	**Had** he been working?	**Had** they been working?
	Yes, I had been working?	Yes, he **had** been working	Yes, they **had** been working.
	No, I **hadn't** been working.	No, he **hadn't** been working.	No, they **hadn't** been working.

CHAPTER 15

The Future Tense

The future tense indicates the time which will come. In other words, it indicates the time of tomorrow. Future tense expresses an action or situation that will occur in the future. This tense is formed by using **will/shall** with the **simple form** of the verb.

- The speaker of the House **will finish** her term in May of 1998.
- The surgeon **is going to perform** the first bypass in Minnesota.
- The president **speaks** tomorrow.

The Simple Future Tense

Use the simple future form of a verb when we are talking about an action that take place in future.

Example: **I will kick** the ball.

I will walk.

Work	**I / you / we / they**	**he / she / it**
Affirmative	I shall/you/we/they will **work**.	He/she/it will **work**.

Negative	I shall/you/we/they **will not work**.	He/she/it **will not work**.
Question	**Shall** I/you/we/they **work**?	**Will** he/she/it **work**?
Short answers	**Will** you **work**?	**Will** she work?
	Yes, I **will**.	Yes, she **will**.
	No, I **will**.	No, she **will**.

The Future Continuous Tense

Use the future continuous form of a verb when you want to talk about a long action that will take place in future. The continuous future is often used to describe what people will do when something else will happen.

Example: I will be playing with ball.

He **will be watching the movie.**

The future continuous is made by having **will** or **shall** + **be** + the verb + **'ing'**.

Example: I will **be** kicking the ball and scor**ing** a goal.

Work	**I**	**he / she / it**	**you / we / they**
Affirmative	I **shall be** working	He **will be** working	They **will be** working
Negative	I **will not be** working	She **will not be** working	We **will not** be working
Question	**Shall** I **be** working?	**Will** he **be** working?	**Will** you **be** working?
Short answers	**Will** you **be** working?	**Will** she **be** working?	**Will** they **be** working?
	Yes, I **was** working.	Yes, she **was** working.	Yes, they **will be** working.
	No, I **will not be** working.	No, she **will not be** working.	No, they **will not be** working.

The Future Perfect Tense

Future perfect tense describes an action that will occur in the future before some other action. This tense is formed by using **will have** with the **past participle** of the verb.

The future perfect tense is made by having **will/shall+ have + verb's 3rd form**.

Work	I	he / she / it	you / we / they
Affirmative	I **shall have** worked	He **will have** worked	They **will have** worked
Negative	I **shall not have** worked	She **will not have** worked	We **will** not have worked
Question	**Shall I** have worked?	**Will** he have worked?	**Will they have** worked?
Short answers	**Will** you have worked?	**Will** he have worked?	**Will they have** worked?
	Yes, I shall have worked.	Yes, he **will have** worked.	Yes, they **will have** worked.
	No, I shall not have worked.	No, he **will not have** worked.	No, they **will not have** worked.

The Future Perfect Continuous Tense

The future perfect continuous tense is used to show that work will have completed in future and still going on. This action describes that people will continuously work for many hours and still they continue it.

The future perfect is made by having **will/shall +have + verb's 1st form** + ing.

	I	he / she / it	you / we / they
Affirmative	I **shall have** been working for 2 hours.	He **will have** been working for 2 hours.	They **will have** been working for 2 hours.
Negative	I **shall not have** been working for 2 hours.	She **will not have been** working for 2 hours.	We will not have **been** working for 2 hours.
Question	**Shall I have** been working for 2 hours?	He **will not have been** working for 2 hours?	He **will not have** been working for 2 hours?

Short answers	**Will have** you been working?	**Will have** he been working?	**Will** he have been working?
	Yes, I will have been working.	Yes, he **will have** been working	Yes, they **will have** been working.
	No, **I will not have** been working.	No, he **will not have** been working.	No, they **will not have** been working.

Chapter 16

Tenses Chart

Simple or Indefinite Tense

		First Person		Second Person		Third Person	
Tense	**Voice**	**Singu-lar**	**Plural**	**Singu-lar**	**Plural**	**Singul-ar**	**Plural**
	Active	I sing a song.	We sing a song.	You sing a song.	You sing a song.	He /she sings a song.	They sing a song.
Present	Passive	A song is sung by me.	A song is sung by us.	A song is sung by you.	A song is sung by you.	A song is sung by him.	A song is sung by them.
	Active	I sang a song.	We sang a song.	You sang a song.	You sang a song.	He/She sang a song.	They sang a song.
Past	Passive	A song was sung by me.	A song were sung by them.	A song were sung by you.	A song were sung by you.	A song was sung by him /her.	A song was sung by them.

Future	Active	I shall sing a song.	We shall sing a song.	You will sing a song.	You will sing a song.	He/ She will sing a song.	They will sing a song.
	Passive	A song shall be sung by me.	A song shall be sung by us.	A song will be sung by you	A song will be sung by you.	A song will be sung by him /her	A song will be sung by them.

Continuous or Progressive Tense

		First Person		**Second Person**		**Third Person**	
Tense	**Voice**	**Singu-lar**	**Plural**	**Singu-lar**	**Plural**	**Singu-lar**	**Plura**
	Active	I am singing a song.	We are singing a song.	You are singing a song.	You are singing a song.	He /she is singing a song.	They are singing a song
Prese-nt	Passive	A song is sung by me.	A song is sung by us.	A song is sung by you.	A song is sung by you.	A song is sung by him.	A song is sung by them
	Active	I was singing a song.	We were singing a song.	You were singing a song	You were singing a song.	He/She is singing a song.	They are singing a song.
	Passive	A song was being sung by me.	A song was being sung by them.	A song was being sung by you.	A song was being sung by you.	A song was being sung by him/h-er.	A song was being sung by them.

Future	Active	I shall be singing a song.	We shall be singing a song.	You will be singing a song.	You will be singing a song.	He/ She will be singing a song.	They will be singing a song.
	Passive	------	------	------	------	------	------

Perfect Tense

		First Person		**Second Person**		**Third Person**	
Tense	**Voice**	**Singu-lar**	**Plural**	**Singu-lar**	**Plural**	**Singu-lar**	**Plural**
	Active	I have sung a song.	We have sung a song.	You have sung a song.	You have sung a song.	He /she has sung a song.	They have sung a song
Prese-nt	Passive	A song has been sung by me.	A song has been sung by us.	A song has been sung by you.	A song has been sung by you.	A song has been sung by him/h-er.	A song has been sung by them.
	Active	I had sung a song.	We had sung a song.	You had sung a song.	You had sung a song.	He/She had sung a song.	They had sung a song.
Past	Passive	A song had been sung by me.	A song had been sung by them.	A song had been sung by you.	A song had been sung by you.	A song had been sung by him/ her.	A song had been sung by them.

Future	Active	I shall have sung a song.	We shall have sung a song.	You will have sung a sung.	You will have sung a song.	He/ She will have sung a song.	They will have sung a song.
	Passive	A song shall have been sung by me.	A song shall have been sung by us.	A song will have been sung by you.	A song will have been sung by you	A song will have been sung by him /her	A song will have been sung by them

Perfect Continuous Tense

		First Person		Second Person		Third Person	
Tense	**Voice**	**Singu-lar**	**Plural**	**Singu-lar**	**Plural**	**Singu-lar**	**Plura**
	Active	I have been singing a song.	We have been singing a song.	You have been singing a song.	You have been singing a song.	He /she has been singing a song.	They have been singing a song
Prese-nt	Passive	------	------	------	------	------	------
	Active	I had been singing a song.	We had been singing a song.	You had been singing a song.	You had been singing a song.	He/She had been singing a song.	They had been singing a song.
Past	Passive	------	------	------	------	------	------

Future	Active	I shall have been singing a song.	We shall have been singing a song.	You will have been singing a song.	You will have been singing a song	He/ She will have been singing a song.	They will have been singing a song.
	Passive	------	------	------	------	------	------

Chapter 17

Rectifying Punctuation

Punctuation is used to create sense, clarity and stress in sentences. Punctuation marks are signals to the readers. In speaking, we can pause, stop, or change our tone of voice.

We can use punctuation marks to structure and organize our writing. The most common of these are the period (or full stop in British English), the comma, the exclamation mark, the question mark, the colon and semi-colon, the quote, the apostrophe, the hyphen and dash, and parentheses and brackets. Capital letters are also used to help us organize meaning and to structure the sense of our writing.

You can quickly see why punctuation is important if you try and read this sentence which has no punctuation at all:

> Perhaps you dont always need to use commas periods colons etc to make sentences clear when i am in a hurry tired cold lazy or angry i sometimes leave out punctuation marks grammar is stupid i can write without it and dont need it my uncle Harry once said he was not very clever and i never

understood a word he wrote to me i think ill learn some punctuation not too much enough to write to Uncle Harry he needs some help

Now let's see how punctuation marks make the difference!

Perhaps you don't always need to use commas, periods, colons etc. to make sentences clear. When I am in a hurry, tired, cold, lazy, or angry I sometimes leave out punctuation marks.

"Grammar is stupid! I can write without it and don't need it," my uncle Harry once said. He was not very clever and I never understood a word he wrote to me. I think I'll learn some punctuation - not too much, enough to write to Uncle Harry. He needs some help!

Always use punctuation marks to make sense of sentence or making sentence understandable.

Punctuations Marks

. Period or Full Stop

? Question Mark

! Exclamation Mark

, Comma

' Apostrophe

"" Quotation Marks

: Colon

; Semicolon

– Dash

- Hyphen

Period [.]

1. Use a period to show the end of a sentence.
   - Hockey is a popular sport in Canada.
2. Use a period after certain abbreviations.
   - The company is located at 888 Bay **St.** in Toronto.
3. Use a period after an initial.
   - **R.S.** Gupta is a wonderful author.
4. Use a period as a decimal point.
   - The boss has given hike of 2.1 percent in salaries.
5. Use a period to separate dollars and cents or rupees.
   - The pen cost **Rs.** 20.30.
6. Use a period after each number in a list printed vertically.
   - For the examples look at the list on this page.

Question Mark [?]

1. Use a question mark at the end of a sentence to show a direct question.
   - How many boys are present in the class?
2. Use a question mark at the end of a declarative statement that you want to emphasize as not believing the statement.
   - She's our new teacher?
3. Use a question mark with parentheses to indicate that you are not sure of a spelling or other fact.
   - I have to visit an orthopedic next week?

Exclamation Mark [!]

1. Use an exclamation mark at the end of a sentence to show surprise or excitement or to indicate strong emotions.
   - The forest is on fire!

- Wow! I never thought Mom would let us go to the concert!

Comma [,]

1. Use a comma to show a pause in a sentence.
   - Therefore, we should write a letter to the prime minister.
2. Use a comma with quotation marks to show what someone has said directly.
   - 'I can come today', she said, 'but not tomorrow.'
3. Use commas for listing three or more different things.
   - Ontario, Quebec, and B.C. are the three biggest provinces.
4. Use commas around relative clauses that add extra information to a sentence.
   - Emily Carr, who was born in 1871, was a great painter.
5. Use a comma after each item in a series of at least three items.
   - I dislike spinach, brinjal and lady finger.
6. Use commas after the street address and city in an address. (Do not use a comma after the state.)
   - The address is 1234 Ansari Road, Darya Ganj, New Delhi– 110002.
7. Use a comma after the day and the year in a date. (No commas are used in dates when using the MLA style.)
   - Connie's birthday is on February 20, 1988.
8. Use a comma to clarify large numbers. Counting from right to left, a comma is needed after every 3 digits. This rule does not apply to years, where no commas are used at all.
   - In 1998 the population of Claremont was 23,899.

9. Use a comma to set off an interruption in the main thought of a sentence.
   - Rosa, of course, will bring her folding chairs.
10. Use a comma after a mild interjection, such as *oh* or well.
    - Oh, the test was not that difficult.
11. Use a comma after the greeting in a personal letter or after closing the letter.
    - Use a comma after the closing of a letter.

Apostrophe [']

1. Use an apostrophe to show ownership of something.
   - This is **David's** computer.

   These are the **player's** things. (things that belong to the player)

Note: For nouns in plural form, put the apostrophe at the end of the noun.

- These are the **players'** things. (things that belong to the players)

2. Use an apostrophe to show letters that have been left out of a word.
   - I **don't** know how to fix it.

Quotation Marks ["]

Use quotation marks to show what someone has said directly.

- The prime minister said, 'We will win the election.'
- 'I can come today', she said, 'but not tomorrow.'

Colon [:]

1. Use a colon to introduce a list of things.
   - There are three positions in hockey: goalie, defence, and forward.

2. Use a colon to introduce a long quotation.
   - The prime minister said: 'We will fight. We will not give up. We will win the next election.'
3. Use a colon between numerals indicating hours and minutes.
   - School starts at 8:05 a.m.
4. Use a colon to introduce a list that appears after an independent clause.
   - You need the following items for class: pencils, pens, paper, rulers, and glue.
5. Use a colon between the title and subtitle of a book.

   Example: *Reading Strategies That Work: Teaching Your Students to Become Better Readers is an excellent resource.*

Semicolon [;]

1. Use a semicolon to join related sentences together.
   - The festival is very popular; people from all over the world visit each year.
2. Use a semicolon in lists that already have commas.
   - The three biggest cities in Canada are Toronto, Ontario; Montreal, Quebec; and Vancouver, B.C.

Dash [—]

1. Use a dash before a phrase that summarizes the idea of a sentence.
   - Mild, wet, and cloudy — these are the characteristics of weather in Vancouver.
2. Use a dash before and after a phrase or list that adds extra information in the middle of a sentence.
   - Most Indians — but not all — voted in the last election.

3. Use a dash to show that someone has been interrupted when speaking.
    - The woman said, 'I want to ask — when the earthquake began to shake the room'.
4. Use a dash to attach an afterthought to an already complete sentence.
    - Sarah bought a new pet yesterday — a boa constrictor.
5. Use a dash after a series of introductory elements.
    - Murder, armed robbery, assault — he has a long list of felonies on his record.

Hyphen [-]

1. Use a hyphen to join two words that form one idea together.
    - sweet-smelling
      fire-resistant
2. Use a hyphen to join prefixes to words.
    - anti-Indian
      non-contact
3. Use a hyphen when writing compound numbers.
    - one-quarter
      twenty-three
4. Use a hyphen to show a family relationship, except 'grand' and 'half.'
    - My sister-in-law helps take care of my great-aunt.
5. Use a hyphen to join a capital letter to a word.
    - I had to have my arm x-rayed.

Brackets ( )

1. Use brackets around words of your own that you add to the words of someone you are quoting.

- The news anchor announced, 'It is my sad duty to inform our audience that we are now at war [with Iraq].'

Underlining (Or Italics)

1. Underline or Italicize titles of long works such as books, magazines, albums, movies, etc. (Do not underline end punctuation.)
   - We use *The Language Handbook* to study grammar.
2. Underline foreign words which are not commonly used in everyday English.
   - If you look closely, you'll see a *pluribus* on most U.S. currency.

CHAPTER 18

Spelling Words

English spelling rules are complex, with many exceptions. If you find spelling to be a particular challenge, here is one strategy to follow:

As a foundation:

- Practice your spellings
- Keep a 'spelling notebook' and list words you commonly misspell or have trouble with
- Keep a list of commonly misspelled words, or words that may be spelled correctly, but misused (Example: who's * whose)
- Keep a list of rules for spelling

Spelling Rules

Here are some basic spelling rules to write correct words and clear confusions.

Spelling Plural Nouns

1. Most words add s to the root forms without any change (barn - barns).

2. Words ending in sh, ch, ss, x, and z, usually add es to form the PLURAL (bush - bushes).
3. Words ending in a consonant and y change the y to i and add es (party - parties).
4. Some words ending in f change the f to v and add es (calf - calves).
5. Some singular words have different words for their plural form (man - men; mouse - mice; goose-geese).

Suffixes

1. A letter or a syllable placed after a word to form a new word is called a suffix. Some suffixes are s, es, ed, ing, er, est, ly, ful, able, ible, ment, ive, ance, ence, ion, tion, ition, ation, sion, ous, ious, less, and al. Sometimes a word will have two suffixes. For example, respectfully has the two suffixes - ful and ly added to the root word respect.
2. Many words are formed by adding ed and ing without any change (furnish - furnished - furnishing).
3. Words ending in a silent e drop the e before adding ed and ing (move - moved - moving).
4. Words ending in a consonant and y change the y to i before adding ed, but do not make any change before adding ing (deny - denied - denying).
5. Words ending in a vowel and y add ed and ing without making any other change (delay - delayed - delaying).

Prefixes

1. A syllable placed before a word to change its meaning is called a prefix. Some prefixes are im, un, in, co, dis, inter.

Doubling the Final Consonant

1. Words of one syllable ending in a single consonant

preceded by a single vowel double the final consonant before adding ed and ing (trim - trimmed - trimming).

2. Words of two or more syllables double the final consonant before adding ed and ing when these conditions are met: the last syllable ends in a single consonant preceded by a single vowel, and the accent is on the last syllable (refer - referred - referring).

Possessive Forms

1. Singular nouns form the possessive by adding an apostrophe and s (pilot - pilot's).
2. Plural nouns that end in s add only an apostrophe to form the possessive (aviators - aviators').
3. Plural nouns that do not end in s add the apostrophe and s to form the possessive (men - men's).

Contractions

1. A word or phrase that has been shortened by leaving out some of the letters is called a contraction.
2. An apostrophe is used to show that the letters have been omitted (won't - will not), (o'clock - of the clock).

Capitals

1. The beginning of a sentence is always capitalized (The day was bright and sunny.).
2. The names of holidays are capitalized (Christmas, Valentine's Day).
3. The names of the months of the year and the days of the week are capitalized (January, Monday).
4. The names of countries are capitalized (United States, Great Britain).

5. An **antonym** is a word that is opposite in meaning to another word. (private -public; good - bad)
6. **Homonyms** are words that are pronounced alike but which are spelled in different ways and have different meanings (knew - new; steel - steal; deer - dear)

Some Special Tips

1. Singular nouns ending with 'ch/sh/s/o/x' take 'es' as the plural form.

Examples:

- Bench-benches
- Brush-brushes
- Class-classes
- Box-boxes
- Potato-potatoes

Some exceptions:

Some of the words ending with 'o' do not take 'es'

Examples:

- Video-videos
- Dynamo-dynamos

2. Singular nouns ending with 'y' take 'ies' as the plural form.

Examples:

- City-cities
- Country-countries
- Lady-ladies

Some exceptions:

If a word contains a vowel before the letter 'y', it does not take 'ies' as its plural form.

Examples:

- Monkey-monkeys
- Toy-toys

3. Singular nouns ending with 'f' or 'fe' take 'ves' as the plural form.

Examples:

- Leaf-leaves
- Calf-calves

Some exceptions:

Some of the words takes only 's' as plural form.

Examples:

- Roof-roofs
- Chief-chiefs

4. Some words have the same form for both singular and plural

Examples:

- Deer-deer
- Fish-fish

5. Some appear like plural but they are singular.

Examples:

- News
- Physics

6. Some words takes different spelling for plural.

Examples:

- Man-men
- Mouse-mice
- Foot-feet

Things to Remember

- ‘**q**’ is always written as ‘**qu**’. It never stands by itself.

  Example: **quick, queen, quarrel**.

- We double ‘**l, f,** and **s**’ after a single short vowel at the end of a word.

  Example: **call, tall, toss, miss, stiff, stuff**.

  Exceptions: **us, bus, gas, if, of, this, yes, plus, nil, pal**.

- Regular plurals are made by adding ‘**s**’.

  Example: **animals, horses, monkeys, and cliffs**.

- **y**’ and not ‘**i**’ is used at the end of an English word and is usually pronounced as a short ‘**i**’.

  Exceptions: **macaroni, spaghetti, vermicelli** (Italian), and **taxi** (short for taxicab).

- A silent ‘**e**’ on the end of a word makes the vowel in front say its own alphabetic name.

  Example: **hate, ride, cube, bake, shire, mare, lobe**.

  Exceptions: **done, come, some, give** and **have**.

- ‘**ck**’ may only be used after a single vowel that does not say its name at the end of a syllable or root word.

  Example: **track, pick, rocket, wreckage**.

- To form plurals of words with a hissing ending, add ‘**es**’

  I.e. after ‘**s, x, z, sh**, and **ch**’

  Example: **buses, foxes, buzzes, wishes** and **churches**.

- Words ending in an ‘**o**’ preceded by a consonant usually add ‘**es**’ to form the plural.

  Example: **potatoes, volcanoes**.

  Exceptions: **pianos, solos, Eskimos**

- Nouns ending in a single '**f**' change the '**f**' to a '**v**' before adding '**es**' to form the plural.

  Example: **leaf – leaves; wolf – wolves.**

  Exceptions: **dwarfs, roofs, chiefs.**

- If a word ends in a consonant plus '**y**', change the '**y**' to and '**i**', before adding any ending. Except: '**ing**'.

  Example: **party – parties;**

  heavy – heaviness

  but; **cry – crying;**

  hurry – hurrying

- When '**w**' comes before '**or**' it often says '**wer**' as '**worm**'.

  Example: **worship, worst, worth, work.**

  Exceptions: **worry, worried, wore.**

- Words ending in both a single vowel and a single consonant always double the last consonant before adding an ending.

  Example: **stop, stopped, stopping.**

  flat, flatter, flattest.

  Exceptions: **fix, box, fox, mix.**

- '**x**' is the same as '**ck**'; that is it counts as a double consonant ending.

- When '**c**' is followed by '**e**', '**i**' or '**y**', it says '**s**'. Otherwise it says '**k**'.

  Example: **centre, ceiling, circle, cycle.**

  cottage, cave, cream, curious, clever.

- When '**g**' is followed by '**i**', '**e**' or '**y**', it says '**j**'. Otherwise it says '**g**' as in gold.

  Example: **gentle, giant, gymnastic.**

  gallon, gold, guide, glass, grow.

Exceptions: **get, got, begin, girl, give, gear, geese, gift, girth, geyser,**

- Drop the final 'e' from a root word before adding an ending beginning with a vowel, but keep it before a consonant.

  Example: **love, loving, lovely.**

  grace, graceful.

- '**ti**', '**ci**' and '**si**' are three spellings most frequently used to say '**sh**' at the beginning of all syllables except the first.

  Example: **national, patient, palatial, infectious.**

  Exceptions: '**ship**' as a suffix, Example: '**worship**'.

- '**i**' comes before '**e**' when it is pronounced '**ee**', except when it follows '**c**' – or when sounding like '**a**' as in '**neighbour**, or **weigh**'.

  Example: **brief, field, priest.**

  Exceptions: **n<u>ei</u>ther, for<u>eig</u>n, sover<u>eig</u>n, s<u>ei</u>zed, counterf<u>ei</u>t, forf<u>ei</u>ted, l<u>ei</u>sure.**

- '**all**' and '**well**' followed by another syllable only have one '**l**'.

  Example: **also, already, although, welcome, welfare.**

- '**full**' and '**till**' joined to another root syllable, drop one '**l**'.

  Example: **useful, cheerful, until.**

- For words ending in a single '**l**' after a single vowel, double the '**l**' before adding a suffix, regardless of accent.

  Example: **cancelled, traveller, signalling, metallic.**

- If a word of <u>more</u> than one syllable ends in a '**t**', preceded by a single vowel, and has the <u>accent</u> on the <u>last</u> syllable, then double the final consonant.

Example: **permit; permitted**.

admit; admitted.

But, if the accent is on the first syllable, don't double the 't'.

Example: **visit; visited.**

- '**ery**' or '**ary**' endings. Words ending in '**ery**' are often obvious.

  Example: **very, brewery, flattery, bakery, nursery**.

  If in doubt, use '**ary**'.

  Example: **dictionary, secretary, commentary, stationary**.

- **ise**', '**ize**' or '**yse**' endings. Most of these words end in '**ise**'.

  Example: **sunrise, surprise, supervise, exercise, disguise, unwise, surmise, advertise**.

  Only two common words end in '**yse**'.

  i.e. **analyse** and **paralyse**.

  Only two common words end in '**ize**'.

  i.e. **prize** and **capsize**.

- '**ceed**', '**sede**' and '**cede**'

  Three '**ceed**' words; **succeed, exceed, proceed.**

  One '**sede**' word; **supersede**.

  All others '**cede**'

  Example: **intercede, antecede, precede**.

- '**able**' or '**ible**' endings.

Use '**able**':

After root words.

Example: **available, dependable**.

After root words ending in 'e'.

Example: **desirable, believable, usable** (drop the 'e').

After 'i'

Example: **reliable, sociable.**

When other forms of the root word have a dominant '**a**' vowel.

Example: **irritable, durable, abominable.**

After a hard 'c' or 'g'.

Example: **educable, practicable, navigable.**

Exceptions: **formidable, inevitable, memorable, probable, portable, indomitable, insuperable.**

Use '**ible**':

After non-root words.

Example: **audible, horrible, possible.**

When the root has an immediate '**ion**' form.

Example: **digestible, suggestible, convertible.**

After a root ending in '**ns**' or '**miss**'.

Example: **responsible, comprehensible, permissible.**

After a soft 'c' or 'g'

Example: **legible, negligible, forcible, invincible.**

Exceptions: **contemptible, resistible, collapsible, flexible.**

Some Examples

The following examples can also help you build your vocabulary and spellings:

accessory *noun*

Spell **accessory** with a double **c** and a double **s**; the ending is **-ory**.

Rule: Change the **-y** to **-ies** to make the plurals of words which end in a consonant plus **-y** (as in *berry/berries*): **accessories**.

accommodate *verb*

Spell **accommodate** with a double **c** and a double **m**; remember that there is an **o** before and after the **m**'s.

Related word: accommodation *noun*

address *noun* and *verb*

Spell **address** with a double **d**.

Example: please **add** your **add**ress.

aggression *noun*

Remember that **aggression** is spelled with a double g and a double s.

Related words: aggressive *adjective* **aggressor** *noun*

alcohol *noun*

Spell **alcohol** with **alco-** at the beginning.

Example: drink **a** large **c**old **o**range juice, not **alco**hol.

allege *verb*

Remember that **allege** has a double **l** and is spelled with **-ege** at the end.

amend *verb*

Remember that **amend** and the related word **amendment** are spelled with a single **m** at the beginning.

apologize or **apologise** *verb*

Spell **apologize** and the related word **apology** with **-olo-** in the middle.

apparent *adjective*

There is a double **p** in **apparent** but only one **r**; the ending is **-ent**.

argument *noun*

There is no **e** after the **u** in **argument**, even though it comes from **argue**. It does not follow the usual rule that the final silent e is kept when adding endings that begin with a consonant.

average *noun* and *verb*

Spell **average** with an **e** after the **v**; the ending is **-age**.

beautiful *adjective*

Remember that **beautiful** and the related words **beauty** and **beautify** are spelled with **beau-** at the beginning.

Example: bare elegant arms are usually **beautiful**.

belief *noun*

Rule: Belief and the related word **believe** follow the rule **i** before **e** except after **c** (as in *thief*).

Related word: believable *adjective*

burglar *noun*

Spell **burglar** with **-lar** at the end.

Related word: burglary *noun*

business *noun*

Remember that **business** begins with **busi-**.

cemetery *noun* (plural **cemeteries**)Remember that **cemetery** ends with **-ery**.

changeable *adjective*

Rule: Keep the final silent **-e** when adding endings which begin with a vowel to words which end in **-ce** or **-ge**

(here, *change*), if this is needed to preserve the soft sound of the first part of the word: **changeable**.

committee *noun*

Spell **committee** with a double **m**, a double **t**, and a double **e** at the end.

consensus *noun*

Remember that **consensus** and the related word **consensual** are spelled with **-sen-** in the middle.

controversy *noun* (plural **controversies**)

Remember that **controversy** is spelled with **-ro-** in the middle.

Example: cont**ro**versy arouses **r**eally **o**pposing views.

Related word: controversial *adjective*

deceive *verb*

Rule: i before **e** except after **c** (as in **receive**).

Related word: deceit *noun*

definite *adjective*

Remember that **definite** ends with **-ite**.

Related word: definitely *adverb*

desperate *adjective*

Spell **desperate** with **-per-** in the middle.

Example: perhaps he was des**per**ate to escape.

disappoint *verb*

Remember that **disappoint** and the related word **disappointment** are spelled with one **s** and a double **p**.

eighth *adjective*

Remember that **eighth** is spelled with **-hth** at the end.

Example: Sam **h**oped **th**at **h**e wouldn't finish eig**hth**.

embarrass *verb*

Remember that **embarrass** and the related word **embarrassment** have a double **r** and a double **s**.

Example: embar**r**a**ss**ed, she was **r**osy **r**ed with **s**evere **s**hame.

extraordinary *adjective*

Spell **extraordinary** with **extra-** at the beginning (it is made up of the words **extra** and **ordinary**).

extreme *adjective* and *noun*

Remember that the ending of **extreme** is spelled **-eme**.

fascinate *verb*

Remember that **fascinate** and the related word **fascination** are spelled with an **s** before the **c**.

fluorescent *adjective*

Remember that **fluorescent** and the related word **fluorescence** begin with **fluor-**.

friend *noun*

Spell **friend** with **-ie-** in the middle.

fulfill *verb*

Spell **fulfill** with one **l** in the middle and one at the end (the spelling **fulfil** is American).

Rule: Double the **l** when adding endings which begin with a vowel to words which end in a vowel plus **l** (as in *travel*): **fulfils, fulfilling, fulfilled**.

Related word: fulfillment *noun*

gauge *noun* and *verb*

Spell **gauge** with **-au-** in the middle (the spelling **gage** is American).

grateful *adjective*

Remember that **grateful** begins with **grate-**.

guarantee *noun* and *verb*

Rule: Although most verbs ending in **-e** drop the final **e** before adding **-ing** (Example: *bake*, *baking*), verbs ending in **-ee**, **-ye**, and **-oe** keep the final **-e**: **guarantees**, **guaranteeing**, **guaranteed**.

harass *verb*

Spell **harass** and the related word **harassment** with a single **r** and a double **s**.

hypocrisy *noun*

Remember that **hypocrisy** begins with **hypo-**; the ending is **-isy**.

Related words: hypocrite *noun* **hypocritical** *adjective*

humorous *adjective*

Rule: When adding certain endings, such as **-ous** and **-ist**, to words that end in **-our** (in this case, *humour*), change **-our** to **-or** before adding the ending: **humorous**; **humorist**.

immediate *adjective*

Spell **immediate** and the related word **immediacy** with a double **m**.

Related word: immediately *adverb*

independent *adjective* and *noun*

Remember that **independent** always ends with **-ent**.

Tip: she's an independ**ent** ag**ent**.

Related word: independence *noun*

installment *noun*

Spell **installment** with one **l** (the spelling **installment** is American).

Rule: Drop the last **l** when adding suffixes (endings) which begin with a consonant to words which end in a double **l** (here, *install*): **instalment.**

itinerary *noun* (plural **itineraries**)

Remember that **itinerary** ends with **-erary**.

liaise *verb*

Remember that **liaise** is spelled with two **i**'s, one before and one after the **a**.

Example: you must liaise with colleagues in Italy and Ireland.

Related word: liaison *noun*

licence *noun*

Do not confuse **licence** with **license**. **Licence** is a noun which means 'a permit to do something' (*a driving licence*), whereas license is a verb meaning 'give a permit to someone: allow something' (*the loggers are licensed to cut mahogany trees*).

In American English, both the noun and the verb are spelled **license**.

lot *pronoun* and *noun*

You should spell **a lot** as two words, not one (*a lot can happen in a month*).

maintenance *noun*

Remember that **maintenance** is spelled with **-ten-** in the middle; the ending is **-ance**.

manoeuvre *noun* and *verb*

Spell **manoeuvre** with **-oeu-** in the middle; the ending is **-re** (the spelling **maneuver** is American).

Related word: manoeuvrable *adjective*

millennium *noun*

Spell **millennium** with a double **l** and a double **n**. The plural can be spelled either **millennia** (like the original Latin) or **millenniums**.

Related word: millennial *adjective*

miniature *noun* and *adjective*

Remember that **miniature** begins with **mini-**.

Example: a **mini**ature **mini**bus.

minuscule *adjective*

Remember that **minuscule** is spelled with a **u** after the **n**.

mischievous *adjective*

Rule: i before **e** except after **c** (as in thief). Remember that **mischievous** ends with **-vous**.

misspell *verb*

Spell **misspell** with a double **s**. The different forms of this verb are: **misspells, misspelling**; the past tense is **misspelt** or **misspelled**.

naive *adjective*

Remember that **naive** is spelled with **-ai-** in the middle. It can also be spelled **naïve**, with two dots over the **i**, as in the original French.

Example: she was naive, with an appealing innocence.

Related word: naivety *noun*

privilege *noun* and *verb*

Remember that **privilege** ends with **-ege**.

questionnaire *noun*

Remember that **questionnaire** (a French word) is spelled with a double **n** and ends with **-aire**.

really *adverb*

Remember that **really** is spelled with a double **l**.

receive *verb*

Rule: i before **e** except after **c**.

recommend *verb*

Spell **recommend** and the related word **recommendation** with a single **c** and a double **m**.

Example: he re**c**o**mm**ended that I **c**ut out **m**ilk and **m**eat from my diet.

restaurant *noun*

Remember that **restaurant** is spelled with **-au-** between the **t** and **r**: it is a French word.

restaurateur *noun*

Although **restaurateur** (a French word) is related to **restaurant**, it is not spelled with an **n** before the second **t**.

rhythm *noun*

Remember that **rhythm** is spelled with **rhy-** at the beginning, then **-thm**.

Example: rhythm really **h**as **y**our **t**wo **h**ips **m**oving.

secretary *noun* (plural **secretaries**)

Spell **secretary** with an **e** after the **r**; the ending is **ary**.

seize *verb*

Remember that **seize** and the related word **seizure** are spelled with the **e** before the **i**: they do not follow the rule of **i** before **e** except after **c**.

separate *verb* and *adjective*

Remember that **separate** is spelled with **-par-** in the middle.

Example: the rock split into two se**par**ate **par**ts.

Related word: separation *noun*

similar *adjective*

Remember that the ending of **similar** is spelled **-lar**.

Related word: similarity *noun* **similarly** *adverb*

skilful *adjective*

Remember that **skilful** is spelled with one **l** in the middle (the spelling **skillful** is American).

Rule: Drop the last **l** when adding suffixes (endings) which begin with a consonant to words which end in a double l (here, **skill** plus **-ful**): **skilful**.

success *noun*

Spell **success** and the related word **successful** with a double **c** and a double s.

Related word: successor *noun*

sufficient *adjective*

Spell **sufficient** with a double **f**; the ending is **-cient**.

suppress *verb*

Spell **suppress** with a double **p** and a double **s**.

surprise *verb* and *noun*

Remember that **surprise** has an **r** before and after the **p**.

Unlike most verbs ending in **-ise**, it cannot be spelled with an **-ize** ending.

threshold *noun*

Remember that **threshold** is spelled with a single **h**.

tomato *noun*

The plural of **tomato** is made by adding **-es**: **tomatoes**.

tomorrow *adverb* and *noun*

Spell **tomorrow** with a single **m** and a double **r**.

Example: tomorrow morning, rise refreshed.

truly *adverb*

Rule: Truly is formed from **true** plus the ending **-ly**; it is one of a group of words in which the final silent **e** is dropped before adding **-ly**.

twelfth *number*

Remember that **twelfth** has an **f** in the middle.

Example: go to the twelfth floor of the building.

unfortunately *adverb*

Spell **unfortunately** with **-ately** at the end (it is made up of the adjective **unfortunate** plus the ending **-ly**).

until *preposition* and *conjunction*

Spell **until** with a single **l**.

vegetarian *noun* and *adjective*

Remember that the beginning of **vegetarian** is spelled **vege-**; the ending is **-arian**.

vehicle *noun*

Spell **vehicle** with **-icle** at the end.

vicious *adjective*

Remember that the beginning of **vicious** is spelled **vici-**.

weird *adjective*

Remember that **weird** is spelled with the **e** before the **i**: it does not follow the usual rule of **i** before **e** except after **c**.

Example: a weird, eerie, inhuman sound.

willful *adjective*

Remember that **willful** is spelled with one **l** in the middle (the spelling **willful** is American).

Rule: Drop the last **l** when adding suffixes (endings) which begin with a consonant to words which end in a double **l** (here, **will** plus **-ful**): **wilful**.

withhold *verb* (withholds, withholding, withheld)

Remember that **withhold** is spelled with a double **h** (it is made up of the words **with** and **hold**)

Words commonly misspelled, or spelled correctly but not used properly:

A: absence, accidentally, accommodation, according, ache, again, against, aisle, allegory, almost, always, although, ancient, airplane, ageing, agonize, apologize

B: beautiful, beginning, believe, body, build, business

C: calendar, consensus, cemetery, coolly, confidence, criticize

D: defendant, disappoint, drunkenness, despair, distance, disguise, difference, describe, decided, double, divide, dilemma, disappear

E: easiness, exceed

F: famous, finish, forest, familiar, from, form

G: guest, guarantee, guilty, government, guardian, gauge

H: halve, happened, here, hear, height, high

I: illegible, indispensable, information, interest, imagine, immediately, independent, instead, irresistible

J: judgment, juice

K: knowledge

L: liquefy, a lot, language, listen, league

M: maintenance, month, mountain, machine, measure, meant, merchandise, memorandum

N: necessary, neither, nighttime

O: occurrence, occasion

P: pastime, paragraph, period, phrase, possible, preferred, pressure, prominent, purchase, purpose, pursue

Q: quite, quiet, queue, questionnaire

R: recommend, receive, region, remember, receipt, reference

S: separate, soldier, sugar, sure, sergeant, says, several, similar, sincerely

T: tyranny, thousands, temperature, thorough, tomorrow, theater, to, two, too, there, their, they're, truly, tournament

U: unfortunately, until, usually, unanimous, unforgettable

V: vacuum, variety, various, vary, vehicle, vicious, village, villain

W: wear, where, we're, weird

Y: yacht, yield

Z: zucchini

Here is yet another list of commonly mispronounced and misspelled words and phrases:

Incorrect	**Correct**
acrossed	across

affidavid	affidavit
Old-timer's disease	Alzheimer's disease
Antartic	Antarctic
Artic	Arctic
aks	ask
athelete, atheletic	athlete, athletic
barbituate	barbiturate
bob wire	barbed wire
bidness	business
a blessing in the skies	a blessing in disguise
calvary	cavalry
cannidate	candidate
card shark	cardsharp
Carpool tunnel syndrome	Carpal tunnel syndrome
caucaphony	cacophony
The Caucases	The Caucasus
chester drawers	chest of drawers
chomp at the bit	champ at the bit
close	clothes
coronet	cornet
dialate	dilate
diptheria	diphtheria
doggy dog world	dog-eat-dog world
drownd	drown
electoral	electoral
excape	escape
expresso	espresso
excetera	et cetera
expecially	especially
Febyuary	February
fedral	federal

fillum	film
fisical	fiscal
flounder	founder
foilage	foliage
For all intensive purposes	For all intents and purposes
forte	fort
Heineken remover	Heimlich maneuver (or manoeuvre, Br.)
heighth	height
'erb	herb
hi-archy	hierarchy
in parenthesis	in parentheses
interpretate	interpret
irregardless	regardless
idn't	isn't
jewlery	jewelry
jist	just
Klu Klux Klan	Ku Klux Klan
lambast	lambaste
larnyx	larynx
laura norder	law and order
leash	lease
libel	liable
libary	library
longlived	long-lived
masonary	masonry
mawv	mauve
mannaise	mayonnaise
miniture	miniature
mute	moot
mis'chievous	mischievous
nother	other

nucular	nuclear
nuptual	nuptial
ofen	often
ordinance	ordnance
orientate	orient
ostensively	ostensibly
Ostraya	Australia
parlament	parliament
perculate	percolate
pottable	potable
perogative	prerogative
perscription	prescription
persnickety	pernickety
preemptory	peremptory
prespire	perspire
plute	pollute
probly, prolly	probably
pronounciation	pronunciation
prostrate	prostate
realator	realtor
revelant	relevant
reoccur	recur
respite	respite
sherbert	sherbet
silicone	silicon
snuck	sneaked
sose	so
spade	spay
spitting image	spit and image
stob	stub
stomp	stamp

suit	suite
supposably	supposedly
supremist	supremacist
tact	tack
take for granite	take for granted
tenant	tenet
tenderhooks	tenterhooks
Tiajuana	Tijuana
triathalon	triathlon
upmost	utmost
verbage	verbiage
volumptuous	voluptuous
wadn't	wasn't
ways	way
wet	whet
yoke	yolk
zuology	zoology

Chapter 19

Confusing Words

There are a few words that sound similar, but have a world of difference in their meaning. Students often get confused with such words. Here is a list of few such words, accompanied by their meaning and usage. Study these words carefully and avoid committing mistakes.

- **accept *vs* except**

Accept is a verb, which means to agree to take something.

Usage: I always **accept** good advice.

Except is a preposition or conjunction, which means not including.

Usage: I teach every day **except** on Sundays.

- **advice *vs* advise**

Advice is a noun, which means an opinion that someone offers you about what you should do or how you should act in a particular situation.

Usage: I need someone to give me some **advice**.

Advise is a verb, which means to give information and suggest types of action.

Usage: I **advise** everybody to be nice to their teacher.

- **affect *vs* effect**

Affect and ***effect*** are two words that are commonly confused.

affect is usually a verb (action) - **effect** is usually a noun (thing)

Hint: If it's something you're going to do, use 'affect.' If it's something you've already done, use 'effect.'

To affect something or someone.

Meaning: to influence, act upon, or change something or someone.

Usage: The noise outside **affected** my performance.

To have an effect on something or someone

Meaning: to have an impact on something or someone.

Usage: His smile had a strange **effect** on me.

Usage: The drug has many adverse side **effects**.

- **alone *vs* lonely**

Alone, can be used as an adjective or adverb. Either use means without other people or on your own.

Usage: He likes living **alone**.

'I think we're **alone** now.' There are just the two of us here.

Lonely is an adjective which means you are unhappy because you are not with other people.

Usage: The house feels **lonely** now that all the children have left home.

- **a lot / alot / allot**

A lot, meaning a large amount or number of people or things, can be used to modify a noun.

Usage:I need **a lot** of time to develop this web site.

It can also be used as an adverb, meaning very much or very often.

Usage: I look **a lot** like my sister.

It has become a common term in speech; and is increasingly used in writing.

Alot does not exist! There is no such word in the English language. If you write it this way – imagine me shouting at you - 'No Such Word!'

Allot is a verb, which means to give (especially a share of something) for a particular purpose:-

Usage: We were allotted a desk each.

- **all ready *vs* already**

All ready means 'completely ready'.

Usage: Are you all ready for the test?

Already is an adverb that means before the present time or earlier than the time expected.

Usage: I asked him to come to the cinema but he'd **already** seen the film.

Or

Are you buying Christmas cards **already**? It's only September!

- **altogether *vs* all together**

All together (adv) means 'together in a single group.'

Usage: The waiter asked if we were **all together**.

Altogether (adv) means 'completely' or 'in total'.

Usage: She wrote less and less often, and eventually she stopped **altogether**.

- **any *vs* some**

Any and ***some*** are both determiners. They are used to talk about indefinite quantities or numbers, when the exact quantity or number is not important. As a general rule we use **some** for positive statements, and **any** for questions and negative statements,

Usage: I asked the barman if he could get me **some** sparkling water. I said, 'Excuse me, have you got **any** sparkling water?' Unfortunately they didn't have **any**.

Usage: Would you mind fetching **some** gummy bears while you're at the shops?

You can also use **any** in a positive statement if it comes after a word whose meaning is negative or limiting:

Usage: A. She gave me **some** bad advice.

B. Really? She rarely gives **any** bad advice.

- **apart *vs* a part**

Apart (adv) separated by distance or time.

Usage: I always feel so lonely when we're **apart**.

A part (noun) a piece of something that forms the whole of something.

Usage: They made me feel like I was **a part** of the family.

- **been *vs* gone**

been is the past participle of **be**

gone is the past participle of **go**

Been is used to describe completed visits. So if you have **been** to England twice, you have travelled there and back twice. If you have **gone** to England, you have not yet returned.

- **beside *vs* besides**

Beside is a preposition of place that means at the side of or next to.

Usage: The house was **beside** the Thames.

besides is an adverb or preposition. It means in addition to or also.

Usage: **Besides** water, we carried some fruit. = 'In addition to water, we carried some fruit.'

- **bored *vs* boring**

bored is an adjective that describes when someone feels tired and unhappy because something is not interesting or because they have nothing to do.

Usage: She was so **bored** that she fell asleep.

boring is an adjective that means something is not interesting or exciting.

Usage: The lesson was so **boring** that she fell asleep.

- **borrow *vs* lend**

To lend:

Meaning: to hand out usually for a certain length of time.

Banks *lend* money.

Libraries *lend* books.

Usage: My mother **lent** me some money, and I must pay her back soon.

- **concentrate *vs* concentrated**

The verb - When you ***concentrate*** you direct all your efforts towards a particular activity, subject or problem.

Usage: You need to **concentrate** harder when you listen to something in another language.

The adjective - If something is ***concentrated*** it means it has had some liquid removed.

Usage: I prefer freshly squeezed orange juice to **concentrated**.

- **council *vs* counsel**

Council is a group noun. It refers to a group of people elected or chosen to make decisions or give advice on a particular subject, to represent a particular group of people, or to run a particular organization.

Usage: 'The local **council** has decided not to allocate any more funds for the project.'

Counsel can be a verb, which means to give advice, especially on social or personal problems.

Usage: She **counsels** the long-term unemployed on how to get a job.

Counsel can also be a noun, which means advice.

Usage: I should have listened to my father's **counsel**, and saved some money instead of spending it all.

- **councillor *vs* counsellor**

Councillor is a noun which means an elected member of a local government.

Usage: He was elected to be a **councillor** in 1998.

Counsellor is a noun, which means someone who is trained to listen to people and give them advice about their problems.

Usage: The student union now employs **a counsellor** to help students with both personal and work-related problems.

- **data *vs* datum**

This isn't so much a common mistake as a common cause for arguments (as is often the case with words of Latin origin).

The dictionaries treat ***data*** as a group noun, meaning information, especially facts or numbers, collected for examination and consideration and used to help decision-making, or meaning information in an electronic form that can be stored and processed by a computer.

Then they go on to confuse matters by giving the following kind of example:-

The ***data was/were*** reviewed before publishing.

So, which is it, ***was*** or ***were***? Strictly speaking '***datum***' is the singular form of and '***data***' is the plural form.

If you're writing for an academic audience, particularly in the sciences, 'data' takes a plural verb.

Usage: The **data are** correct.

But *most* people treat '***data***' as a singular noun, especially when talking about computers etc.

Usage: The **data is** being transferred from my computer to yours.

- **discreet *vs* discrete**

Discreet is an adjective.

It means to be careful or modest, not to cause embarrassment or attract too much attention, especially by keeping something secret.

Usage: To work for the royal family you have to be very **discreet**.

Discrete is an adjective.

It means something is distinct and separate or has a clear independent shape or form.

Usage: She painted using strong colours, **discrete** shapes, and rhythmic patterns.

- **don't have to *vs* mustn't**

Don't have to = Do not have to We have to use ***don't have to*** to say that there is no obligation or necessity to do something.

Usage: You **don't have to** do the exercises at the end of this page.

Mustn't = must not is a modal verb used to show that something is not allowed. When you use ***mustn't*** you are telling people not to do things. It has the same force as ***don't*** , as in: ***Don't do that!***

Usage: You **mustn't** drink if you're going to drive.

- **downside *vs* underside**

Downside is a noun that means the disadvantage of a situation.

Usage: One of the **downsides** of living in London, of course, is that it is very expensive.

Underside is a noun that means the side of something that is usually nearest the ground.

Usage: Look at the **underside** of your iMac display. If you see an Ambient Light Sensor, you have a second generation iMac G5.

- **either *vs* as well / too**

Either is used with a negative verb when you are agreeing with something someone doesn't do or like etc.

Usage: B agrees with A in the negative

A - I don't like cheese.' B - 'I don't like it **either**.

A- I haven't seen Lord of the Rings. B - I haven't seen it **either**.

As well / Too are used with an affirmative verb when you are agreeing with something someone does or likes etc.

Usage: B agrees with A in the positive

A - I love ice cream. B - I love it **too**. / I love it **as well**.

A- I've seen Gladiator. B - I've seen it **too**. / I've seen it **as well**.

- **every day *vs* everyday**

Every day - here every is a determiner and day is a noun.

When you say every day you mean each day without exception.

Usage: You have been late for school **every day** this week.

Everyday is an adjective.

When you say everyday you mean ordinary, unremarkable.

Usage: My culture pages offer an insight into the **everyday** life of Britain.

- **excited *vs* exciting**

Excited is an adjective that describes when someone feels happy and enthusiastic about something.

Usage: She was so **excited** that she couldn't sleep.

Exciting is an adjective that means something is making you excited.

Usage: The football match was so **exciting** that she couldn't wait to tell everyone about it.

- **experience *vs* experience(s)**

Experience can be an uncountable noun. You use it when

you're talking about knowledge or skill which is obtained from doing, seeing or feeling things.

Usage: Do you have any **experience** of working internationally?

Experience(s) can be a countable noun. You use it when you are talking about a particular incident or incidents that affect you.

Usage: It was interesting hearing about his **experiences** during the war.

Experience can also be a verb. It means something that happens to you, or something you feel.

Usage: When I first moved to Germany **I experienced** a lot of problems.

- **fewer *vs* less**

Everyone gets this wrong – including native speakers. The general rule is to use **fewer** for things you can count (individually), and **less** for things you can only measure

Usage: There were **fewer** days below freezing last winter. (Days can be counted.)

I drink **less** coffee than she does. (Coffee cannot be counted individually it has to be measured).

- **for *vs* since**

The prepositions ***for*** and ***since*** are often used with time expressions.

For indicates a period of time.

Usage: I have been working here **for** 2 years.

Since indicates a point in time.

Usage: I have been working here **since** the year before last.

- **good** ***vs*** **well**

Good is an adjective. We use good when we want to give more information about a noun.

Usage: My dog Sam is very **good**. He's a **good** dog.

She didn't speak very **good** English. Her English isn't very **good**.

Well is usually used as an adverb. We use well when we want to give more information about a verb.

Usage: He usually behaves very **well**.

She didn't speak English very **well**.

Usage: She wasn't a **well** woman.

and when you describe sensations:

Usage: This pizza tastes/smells/ looks **good**.

If you say 'You look ***good***.' It means they look attractive.

If you say 'You look ***well***.' It means they look healthy.

- **hear** ***vs*** **listen**

hear is a verb that means to receive or become aware of a sound using your ears, so you don't have to make an effort in order to just hear something.

Usage: She **heard** some noise outside.

listen is a verb that means to give attention to someone or something in order to hear them, so you make an make an effort in order to hear something properly.

Usage: She **listened** to the noise and realised it was only a cat.

- **heroin** ***vs*** **heroine**

Heroin is a noun, it is a powerful illegal drug, obtained from morphine and is extremely addictive.

Usage: He was arrested for supplying heroin, a class A drug.

Heroine is a female person who is admired for having done something very brave or having achieved something great. The male equivalent is hero.

Usage: Grace Darling is one of England's best known **heroines**.

- **he's *vs* his**

He's is the short form of 'he is' or 'he has'.

Usage: Don't be scared – **he's** very friendly.

His is a possesive pronoun, it is used to show something belonging to or connected with a man, boy or male animal that has just been mentioned.

Usage: Mark just phoned to say he'd left his coat behind. Do you know if this is **his**?

- **'How do you do?' *vs* 'How are you?'**

How do you do?

This **is not** a question. It is another, very formal way of saying **'Hello.'** It is also very British.

The correct response is; 'Pleased to meet you.' or 'How do you do.' or just 'Hello.'

We only really use it the **first time** we meet someone.

How are you?

This **is** a question.

A polite response is; 'I'm fine thanks. And you?'

- **I *vs* me**

Usually we choose the correct form by instinct.

For example:

I am a teacher. (not **me**)

Give that to **me**. (not **I**)

There are other times when people make mistakes with these two pronouns. **I/me** is difficult when it is coupled with another pronoun or with a noun. This is when you have to think about the subject/object in a sentence.

For example:

It was **I** who did the homework.

Or

It was **me** who did the homework.

Make the statement simpler:-

'**I** did the homework.' so 'It was **I** who did the homework', is correct.

The teacher gave the homework to my friend and **me**. (Not **I**)

- **interested *vs* interesting**

Interested is a past participle. When used as an adjective it says how someone feels.

Usage: I was very **interested** in the lesson.

Interesting is a present participle. When used as an adjective it describes the people or things that cause the feelings.

Usage: It was an **interesting** lesson.

- **lay *vs* lie**

Lay is an irregular transitive verb (lay / laid/ laid / laying). It needs a direct object. It means to put something or someone down (often in a horizontal position).

Usage: '**Lay** your head on the pillow.'

Lie is an irregular intransitive verb (lie / lay / laid / lying). It does not take a direct object. It means to rest in a horizontal position or to be located somewhere.

Usage: If you are tired **lie** here and have a rest.

Nottingham **lies** in the Midlands.

- **lay down *vs* lie down**

Lay down has several different meanings.

If you lay something down it can mean you officially establish a rule, or officially state the way in which something should be done.

Usage: Please follow the rules **laid down** by the administrator.

If you lay something down your weapons it means you stop fighting.

Usage: They **laid down** their guns and surrendered.

If you lay wine down it means you are storing it for drinking in the future.

Usage: I **laid down** this bottle in 1998. It should be perfect for drinking now.

Lie down means to move into a position in which your body is flat, usually in order to sleep or rest.

Usage: If you are tired **lie down** and have a rest.

- **look after *vs* look for**

To look after; means to take care of or be in charge of something or someone.

Usage: I often ask my mother to **look after** the children.

To look for; means to try to find something or someone.

Usage: I am **looking for** my keys. Have you seen them?

- **look at *vs* watch**

In this context ***look*** is usually followed by the preposition ***at***.

When you ***look at*** someone or something you are interested in the appearance.

Generally we ***look at*** things that are static.

Usage: **Look at** these photos, they're really good.

I went to the art gallery to **look at** the exhibition of paintings.

Watch is a verb.

When you ***watch*** someone or something you are interested in what happens.

Generally we ***watch*** things that move or change state.

Usage: I **watch** TV every night.

The security guard **watched** the shoplifter steal the clock.

- **look over *vs* overlook**

Look over is a phrasal verb.

When you ***look over*** something or someone you quickly examine it or them.

Usage: I asked my teacher to **look over** what I had written.

Overlook is a verb.

When you ***overlook*** someone or something you fail to notice or consider it or them.

Usage: I think my teacher **overlooked** some of my mistakes.

- **loose *vs* lose**

Loose is an adjective. If something isn't fixed properly or it doesn't fit, because it's too large, it's loose.

Usage: My headphones weren't working because a wire was **loose**.

Lose is a verb that means to no longer possess something because you do not know where it is, or because it has been taken away from you.

Usage: A lot of people will **lose** their job if there is a recession.

- **nor *vs* or**

nor (conjunction) is always used in the negative, usually before the second or last of a set of negative possibilities, after 'neither'.

Usage: He drinks neither wine **nor** beer.

or (conjunction) is used to connect different possibilities.

Usage: Is it Tuesday **or** Wednesday today?

- **me *vs* my**

As in **I *vs* me** we usually choose the correct form by instinct.

Me is used as the object of a verb or preposition. You use me to refer to yourself.

In short answers, we usually use this form.

Usage: 'Who's there?' ~ **'It's me!'**

'I want to buy that new DVD.' ~ **'Me too!'**

My is a possessive adjective.

Usage: **My** mother loves me.

Now consider the following sentences:-

'I'm going to **me** and Margaret's room.' or 'I'm going to **my** and Margaret's room.'

Which is correct? 'Me' or 'My'?

Simplify the sentence by removing the second person:-

'I'm going to ***my*** room.' So, 'I'm going to **my** and Margaret's room', is correct.

A real point of confusion arises when considering the use of '**my**' or '**me**' as the 'subject' of a gerund.

The teacher didn't like **me** telling jokes in class.

The teacher didn't like **my** telling jokes in class.

But which is correct? Well they both are - sort of, but the use of the possessive, '***my telling jokes in class*** ' serves to isolate the telling of jokes as the object of my teacher's anger. It's hopefully not '**me**' at whom she/he has become upset, but the telling of jokes. In the sentence, '***me telling jokes in class***', it might seem as though the teacher doesn't like **me** personally. The *rule* is that the subject of a gerund is supposed to be in the possessive case.

Remember though that this is a purists view. Both are now becoming acceptable through common usage. However, you can avoid any confusion by writing the sentence in a different way:-

The teacher didn't like the way I told jokes in class.

- **most *vs* the most**

Most without an article is usually used as an adjective, which means almost all.

Usage:

They ate **most** of the cake.

Most days I go for a jog.

The most is usually used to form the superlative of many adjectives and adverbs.

Usage: Paul earns **the most** money.

The Miss World competition is held every year to find **the most** beautiful woman in the world.

- **overtake *vs* takeover / take over**

Overtake is a verb.

It can mean to go beyond something by being better, or if you're driving to come from behind another vehicle or a person and move in front of it.

Usage: You should always check your rear view mirror before you **overtake** another car.

Takeover as a noun is used when one organisation gains control of a company by buying most of its shares.

Usage: In September 2006 Merck announced their **takeover** of Serono SA.

Take over as a phrasal verb means to get control of a company by buying most of its shares.

Usage: Merck finally took Serono over in 2007.

- **personal *vs* personnel**

Personal is an adjective.

It can mean relating to or belonging to someone.

Usage: Your **personal** belongings are the things that belong to you.

It can relate to the private parts of someone's life, including their relationships and feelings.

Usage: If you have **personal** problems, it means you have problems that are private and sensitive to you. Perhaps problems in a relationship.

It can also mean something that is designed for or used by one person.

Usage: a **personal** computer or stereo.

And it can relate to your body

Usage: when talk about **personal** hygiene.

Personnel is a noun.

The people who work for an organisation are the personnel.

Usage: Military **personnel** are the members of an army.

The department of an organisation that deals with finding people to work there, keeping records about them, etc is the Personnel Department. The head of that department is the Personnel Manager.

Usage: I need to speak to someone in **Personnel**.

- **practice *vs* practise**

Practice is a noun

Usage: We need to put these ideas into **practice**.

Practise is a verb

Usage: To learn English well you have to **practise**.

- **principal *vs* principle**

Principal as an adjective means first in order of importance:

Usage: The Mississippi is the **principal** river of the United States.

Principal as a noun can mean the head teacher in a school or college:

Usage: The teacher sent the unruly student to see the **principal**.

Principal as a noun can also mean the original amount of a debt on which interest is calculated.

- **to see *vs* to watch**

To see means to be aware of what is around you by using your eyes.

Usage: I can **see** the smoke from here.

To watch means to look at something for a period of time, especially something that is changing or moving.

Usage: I **watched** the cricket match.

- **shortage *vs* shortness**

Shortage is a noun meaning when there is not enough of something.

Usage: There is a **shortage** of skilled workers in the industry.

Shortness is a also a noun meaning the condition of being short spatially.

Usage: **Shortness** in children and young adults nearly always results from below-average growth in childhood.

- **so *vs* such**

So when used as in front of an adjective or an adverb means very.

Usage: My English teacher is **so** patient. She teaches us **so** well.

Such when used as a determiner can be used in front of a noun or an adjective and a noun to show extremes, you can't use it in front of adverbs.

Usage: She is **such** a patient teacher.

- **stationary *vs* stationery**

Stationary means standing still or not moving

Usage: The car was **stationary**.

Stationery means the items needed for writing, such as paper, pens, pencils and envelopes.

Usage: It is the secretary's job to order the **stationery**?

- **take care *vs* take care of**

Take care is used when saying goodbye to someone. It actually means 'Take care *of yourself*.'

Usage: Bye! **Take care.**

Take care of means to look after someone or something:

Usage: You should **take care of** your new car, it cost a lot of money.

- **that, which, who**

'***Who***' (or ***whom***) is a pronoun, and is used as the subject or object of a verb to show which person you are referring to, or to add information about a person just mentioned. It is used for people, not things.

'***Which***' is a pronoun, and is used as the subject or object of a verb to show what thing or things you are referring to, or to add information about the thing just mentioned. It is used for things, not people.

'***That***' is a pronoun, and is used as the subject or object of a verb to show which person or thing you are referring to, or to add information about a person or thing just mentioned. It can be used for people and things. It can sometimes be omitted.

Usage:

The girl **who** was hungry.

The boy **whom** I talked to.

The dog **that** wagged its tail.

The software (**that**) I wrote.

The company, **which / that** hired me.

- **there, their, they're**

There can be used as an adjective of place:

Usage: The car is over **there** in the car park.

There can also be used as the introductory subject in sentences:-

Usage: **There** are some grammar pages on this web site.

They're is the a contraction of 'they are'.

Usage: **They're** always surfing the Internet.

Their is a possessive pronoun like 'her' or 'our'.

Usage: Have **they** done **their** homework?

Example: **There's** a large family in this town. Look **they're** over **there** by **their** car.'

- **trainee *vs* trainer**

A trainee is a person who is learning and practising the skills of a particular job.

Usage: There is a shortage of **trainee** dentists in the UK.

A trainer is a person who teaches skills for a particular job, activity or sport.

Usage: I like to think of myself as an English **trainer**, not an English teacher.

- **to, too or two?**

To is the most common form. When to is used before a verb it forms part of the infiinitive:

Usage: I need **to** visit the dentist.

To is also a preposition, often used to indicate direction, which begins a prepositional phrase.

Usage: I need to go **to** the dentist.

Too is an adjective meaning 'extra or more than necessary' after all it has 2 Os - 1 too many?

Usage: The film was **too** long.

Too is also an adjective meaning 'also'.

Usage: I thought it was too long, **too**.

Two is a number.

Usage: I only drank **two** pints of beer.

More examples: We went **to** a football match. (preposition)

We like **to** watch a good film. (infinitive)

We ate **too** much. (meaning 'excessively')

I like baseball, **too**. (meaning 'also')

Six divided by three is **two**. (number)

They own **two** cars. (number)

- **travel, trip voyage or journey?**

Travel (v) is used in general terms as a verb – it usually means to change location. The word travel is very rarely used as a noun.

Usage: I have to **travel** a lot for work.

Trip (n) is often substituted for the word 'holiday' when the travelling distance was short.

Usage: How was your **trip**?

It is often used in connection with business.

Usage: I have to travel a lot for work. I am off on another **business trip** next week.

Trip (v) has a totally different meaning. It means to nearly fall over.

Usage: I **tripped** over the carpet and sprained my ankle.

Voyage (n) is usually a long journey by boat. The word voyage is very rarely used as a verb.

Usage: The **voyage** to South Africa took over six weeks.

Journey (n) is used more in British English than American English. It means the 'piece' of travel between two or more points. The word journey is very rarely used as a verb.

Usage: The **journey** from Darmstadt to Nottingham takes 12 hours.

- **used to *vs* used to do**

Used to can be used as an adjective and we use it to talk about things that have become familiar, and are no longer strange or new.

Usage: I am **used to** mistakes now.

You can also be used to doing something.

Usage: I am **used to** making mistakes now.

Used to do - If we say something used to happen we are talking about repeated events and actions in the past, usually things that happened a long time ago and are now finished.

Usage: I **used to** smoke.

- **what *vs* which**

Which and *what* are both used in questions:-

What is used to ask a question when there are an unknown number or infinite possibilities for an answer. You know that there are many, many ways that exist to address your question, and you want to find out — from all those possibilities that you might not even know about — the best way.

Usage: **What** movie did you go to see?

Which is used if you are choosing between two items, already defined, in a different sentence, like this:

Usage: **Which** shoes should I wear with this dress — my blue ones or my black ones?

You can use which when you have a very small or limited field to choose from. Certainly use which, not what, when there are only two choices, or if both speaker and listener can visualize all the items under consideration:

Usage: **Which** foot did you break?

Often, either which or what can be used for several choices, depending on what is in the speaker's mind:

Usage:

A- **Which** bus goes to the centre?

B - **What** bus shall I take?

Both sentences are fine. The speaker is probably thinking about fewer buses in sentence (a) than in sentence (b).

- **who *vs* whom**

Who is used as the subject of a verb. Basically anytime 'I', 'she' or 'he' 'feels' right, ***who*** can be used.

Usage: She is the one **who** built that funny English website.

In questions ***who*** is used when asking which person or people did something, or when asking what someone's name is. In fact in informal writing and speech ***who*** is used most of the time.

Usage:

Who is that girl over there?

Who let the dogs out?

She asked me if I knew ***who*** *had got the job.*

Whom *is* used in formal writing as the object of a verb or preposition.

Usage: He took out a photo of his son, **whom** he adores.

There were 500 passengers, of ***whom*** *121 drowned.*

Chapter 20

Rectify Sentences

Now that you have learnt the rules of grammar and spelling, have a look at some of the commonly made mistakes and their corrections:

Incorrect Sentence:	I am difficult to learn English.
Correct Sentence:	It is difficult for me to learn English.
Incorrect Sentence:	Uncle's advice is great significance.
Correct Sentence:	Uncle's advice is of great significance.
Incorrect Sentence:	Seems nothing changed to me.
Correct Sentence:	It seems that nothing has changed.
Incorrect Sentence:	My telephone conversation with you for past one and half week has made me feel you as a very firm character.
Correct Sentence:	Having telephoned with you for one week, I think you have a very firm/strong character.
Incorrect Sentence:	I am going to a picnic.
Correct Sentence:	I am going on a picnic.

Incorrect Sentence:	He succeeded to get the prize.
Correct Sentence:	He succeeded in getting the prize.
Incorrect Sentence:	I am a bit in a hurry.
Correct Sentence:	I am in a bit of a hurry.
Incorrect Sentence:	His room's windows are open.
Correct Sentence:	The windows of his room are open.
Incorrect Sentence:	I enjoyed during thc holidays.
Correct Sentence:	I enjoyed myself during the holidays.
Incorrect Sentence:	How many mountains exist in Australia?
Correct Sentence:	How many mountains are there in Australia?
Incorrect Sentence:	I had told you I am from Africa.
Correct Sentence:	I have told you before that I am from Africa.
Incorrect Sentence:	Why you want to know more about me? I am just a small people.
Correct Sentence:	Why do you want to know more about me? I am a nobody.
Incorrect Sentence:	How do you think to learn the English?
Correct Sentence:	What is your point on learning English?
Incorrect Sentence:	I am no exceptional.
Correct Sentence:	I am no exception.
Incorrect Sentence:	Can you join me the talk?
Correct Sentence:	Can I join the talk?
Incorrect Sentence:	The blue is my favourite colour.
Correct Sentence:	Blue is my favourite colour.

Incorrect Sentence: I'm heard music.

Correct Sentence: I am listening to some music now.

Incorrect Sentence: Do you live there from the day your born.

Correct Sentence: Have you lived there since birth?

Incorrect Sentence: My house is to ten minute of her.

Correct Sentence: It is a ten minute drive from my house to hers.

Incorrect Sentence: Betty, are you investing on stock market?

Correct Sentence: Betty, are you investing in the stock market?

Incorrect Sentence: I am going to watch the cinema tonight.

Correct Sentence: I am going to a movie tonight.

Incorrect Sentence: I am come from America.

Correct Sentence: I am from America/ I come from America.

Incorrect Sentence: I still so surprise we were born in same day.

Correct Sentence: I am so surprised that we were born on the same day.

Incorrect Sentence: We will tolerate no interference with our internal affairs.

Correct Sentence: We will tolerate no interference in our internal affairs.

Incorrect Sentence: What is the difference of these two things?

Correct Sentence: What is the difference between these two things?

Incorrect Sentence:	I'm also from China, but I'm live in Philippines now.
Correct Sentence:	I'm also from China, but I'm living in the Philippines now.
Incorrect Sentence:	What hobby do you like?
Correct Sentence:	What is your hobby?
Incorrect Sentence:	Almost people here I never met before.
Correct Sentence:	Almost all the people here are strangers to me.
Incorrect Sentence:	He went to abroad to further his study.
Correct Sentence:	He went abroad to further his study.
Incorrect Sentence:	You must be quite a character.
Correct Sentence:	You are quite a character.
Incorrect Sentence:	Which kind of car?
Correct Sentence:	What type of car?
Incorrect Sentence:	I am so boring today, please bring me fun.
Correct Sentence:	I feel so bored today, please say something funny.
Incorrect Sentence:	More police was sent to the scene of the crime.
Correct Sentence:	More police were sent to the scene of the crime.
Incorrect Sentence:	The team bring a lot of happy for football fan in the world but now I doubtful them.
Correct Sentence:	The team used to bring a lot of fun to the soccer fans in the world, but I am doubtful of them now.

Incorrect Sentence:	I wonder have you be teacher before !
Correct Sentence:	I wonder if you were a teacher before!
Incorrect Sentence:	Under the help of an influential friend, he got the job.
Correct Sentence:	With the help of an influential friend, he got the job.
Incorrect Sentence:	You may not realize that how important time is.
Correct Sentence:	You may not realize how important time is.
Incorrect Sentence:	You can try it more.
Correct Sentence:	You can try a few times.
Incorrect Sentence:	Make sure that it is a high pay job.
Correct Sentence:	Make sure that it is a high paying job.
Incorrect Sentence:	Because that can let me more to be clear about your talk.
Correct Sentence:	Because that can help me to understand what you said better.
Incorrect Sentence:	Kitty, your honey was left just now because I told him you will coming soon.
Correct Sentence:	Kitty, your honey has just left as I told him you would be coming soon.
Incorrect Sentence:	I don't have a forum. And I also don't know how to make it too.
Correct Sentence:	I don't have a forum. And I also don't know how to make one either.
Incorrect Sentence:	Give me a favour!
Correct Sentence:	Please do me a favour!

Incorrect Sentence:	You are very learned.
Correct Sentence:	You are very knowledgeable.
Incorrect Sentence:	Then I was left this company found a another job.
Correct Sentence:	Then I left this company and found another job.
Incorrect Sentence:	You're not get used to it, I guess!
Correct Sentence:	You're not used to it, I guess!
Incorrect Sentence:	Well, now my connection have problem.
Correct Sentence:	Well, I have some problems with my connection now.
Incorrect Sentence:	But you know a lot about computer, isn't it? I know nothing at all about it !
Correct Sentence:	But you know a lot about computer, don't you? I myself know nothing about it!
Incorrect Sentence:	I writed the sentences yours down, Maggie.
Correct Sentence:	I have written down your sentences, Maggie.
Incorrect Sentence:	The India is coming into rainy weather.
Correct Sentence:	India is in rainy season now.
Incorrect Sentence:	John said that, "I know the answer."
Correct Sentence:	John said, "I know the answer."
Incorrect Sentence:	Well, Peter!!! You must not a material boy, that is my kind too.
Correct Sentence:	Well, Peter!!! You are not a materialistic person like me.

Incorrect Sentence:	I am living at Canada now, and working as a sales.
Correct Sentence:	I am living in Canada now and working in sales. Or I am living in Canada now and working as a sales representative.
Incorrect Sentence:	But I had sent it for 3 days.
Correct Sentence:	But I sent it three days ago.
Incorrect Sentence:	I do not like English, so, I will go out here.
Correct Sentence:	I don't like English, so I am leaving now.
Incorrect Sentence:	Either of them are to go.
Correct Sentence:	Either of them is to go.
Incorrect Sentence:	But you know a lot about computer, isn't it? I know nothing at all about it!
Correct Sentence:	But you know a lot about computer, don't you? I myself know nothing about it!
Incorrect Sentence:	John is kindness, so many people want to chat with him.
Correct Sentence:	John is so kind that many people want to chat with him.
Incorrect Sentence:	How was your sleeping yesterday? Henry.
Correct Sentence:	Did you have a good sleep yesterday, Henry?
Incorrect Sentence:	She told me there is no another way.
Correct Sentence:	She told me there was no other way.
Incorrect Sentence:	Why are you come here so often?
Correct Sentence:	Why do you come here so often?

Incorrect Sentence: Are you born in Japan?

Correct Sentence: Were you born in Japan?

Incorrect Sentence: My sister she is at school.

Correct Sentence: My sister is at school.

Incorrect Sentence: He was in a hospital, and he is recently out of it.

Correct Sentence: He was discharged from the hospital recently.

Incorrect Sentence: How many days left for you to quit your position?

Correct Sentence: How many days are left before you quit your job? Or

How many days are left until you quit your job?

Incorrect Sentence: We were astonished by his sudden resignation.

Correct Sentence: We were astonished at his sudden resignation.

Incorrect Sentence: But chat room of teacher with this chat room are difference. Right?

Correct Sentence: But there is difference between the teacher's chat room and this chat room, right?

Incorrect Sentence: In fact, Billy really owns some personality to be a VIP.

Correct Sentence: In fact, Billy really has what it takes to be a VIP.

Incorrect Sentence: I have not 2 years meet him.

Correct Sentence: I haven't met him for two years.

Incorrect Sentence:	Seems nothing changed to me.
Correct Sentence:	It seems that nothing has changed to me. Or It seems that nothing has changed in me.
Incorrect Sentence:	We have lots of rain, because we're in monsoon season.
Correct Sentence:	There is a lot of rain here as we are in monsoon season now.
Incorrect Sentence:	How much is the temperature?
Correct Sentence:	What is the temperature?
Incorrect Sentence:	Why not come yesterday?
Correct Sentence:	Why didn't you come yesterday?
Incorrect Sentence:	Don't feel anger with me!!! I'm just kidding.
Correct Sentence:	Don't be mad at me !!! I'm just kidding.
Incorrect Sentence:	I don't know how speak it in English.
Correct Sentence:	I don't know how to say it in English.
Incorrect Sentence:	I am a Chinese and have been abroad 10 years.
Correct Sentence:	I am Chinese and have been in abroad for ten years.
Incorrect Sentence:	I wonder if there is a comment on the certificate by GE about how good a student perform in the course?
Correct Sentence:	I wonder if there is a comment on the certificate by GE about how well a student performs in the course?
Incorrect Sentence:	OK, tell me how does he like?
Correct Sentence:	OK, tell me what he looks like?

Incorrect Sentence: Tom sent his picture to me for long time ago.

Correct Sentence: Tom sent me his picture a long time ago.

Incorrect Sentence: I think you should go to abroad find a job make your life a little bit changed.

Correct Sentence: I think you should go abroad to find a job and make your life a little bit different for a change.

Incorrect Sentence: Lilian is living far away with Egypt.

Correct Sentence: Lilian is living far away from Egypt.

Incorrect Sentence: Are you a saler, Alvin?

Correct Sentence: Are you a salesman, Alvin?

Incorrect Sentence: Would you please don't ask me this question, OK?

Correct Sentence: Would you please not ask me this question, OK?

Incorrect Sentence: I can't follow you two talk now.

Correct Sentence: I can't follow what both of you are talking about.

Incorrect Sentence: I think your qualification will surely make you open a computer or English training center.

Correct Sentence: I think you can open up a computer or English training center with your qualifications.

Incorrect Sentence: You must know she is jealous very much.

Correct Sentence: You must know that she is jealous by nature.

Incorrect Sentence: Do you like your female staff flirted you when you be a boss?

Correct Sentence: Would you mind if your staff flirted with you if you were the boss?

Incorrect Sentence: Today is very slow.

Correct Sentence: The connection is slow today.

Incorrect Sentence: Today, I'll wash my cat.

Correct Sentence: I'll give my cat a bath today.

Incorrect Sentence: When children grow up, they are sent to the school.

Correct Sentence: When children grow up, they are sent to school.

Incorrect Sentence: We have lots of rain, because we're in monsoon season.

Correct Sentence: There is a lot of rain here as we are in monsoon season now.

Incorrect Sentence: The farm can't also be escaped from that typhoon.

Correct Sentence: The typhoon has caused great damage on the farm.

Incorrect Sentence: I think your express will have a little difficult, but that is a lucky thing, I can understand you.

Correct Sentence: I think you have difficulty in expressing your idea. Luckily, I can understand you.

Incorrect Sentence: I am sure not even one man can control himself if he meet this kind of situation.

Correct Sentence: I doubt that there is even one man who can control himself in this situation.

Incorrect Sentence:	How are you this week?
Correct Sentence:	How have you been this week?
Incorrect Sentence:	If one day I am good in English, I would definitely admit it.
Correct Sentence:	If someday I am good at English, I will definitely admit it.
Incorrect Sentence:	I know you are good in computer and English.
Correct Sentence:	I know you are good at computers/ computing and English.
Incorrect Sentence:	I wish I have .....
Correct Sentence:	I wish I had ....
Incorrect Sentence:	It is easy or not get visa?
Correct Sentence:	Is it easy to get visa?
Incorrect Sentence:	The company, having finished the construction project, it received its pay.
Correct Sentence:	The company, having finished the construction project, received its pay.
Incorrect Sentence:	He will be great help for you.
Correct Sentence:	He will be of great help to you.
Incorrect Sentence:	What sport are you interest?
Correct Sentence:	What sports are you interested in?
Incorrect Sentence:	What time of a day now in your country?
Correct Sentence:	What is the time now in your country?
Incorrect Sentence:	Should we continuous our speak in English language?
Correct Sentence:	Shall we continue speaking in English?

Incorrect Sentence: I have been many places in Beijing. I like this city so much.

Correct Sentence: I have been to many places in Beijing. I like this city very much.

Incorrect Sentence: Where is the students come from?

Correct Sentence: Where do the students come from?

Incorrect Sentence: Chan, are your work busy?

Correct Sentence: Chan, do you have a busy job?

Incorrect Sentence: How long does the news?

Correct Sentence: How long does the news last?

Incorrect Sentence: Some of the students speak the Mandarin very well.

Correct Sentence: Some of the students speak Mandarin very well.

Incorrect Sentence: Come to here is more easy for you.

Correct Sentence: If you come here it will be easier for you.

Incorrect Sentence: Professor Li will speak on the latest development in the chemistry.

Correct Sentence: Professor Li will speak on the latest development in Chemistry.

Incorrect Sentence: I was/got cancelled our date by her?

Correct Sentence: She cancelled the date.

Incorrect Sentence: We have full off and half off on Sunday.

Correct Sentence: We are given the option to work either full or half day on Sunday.

Incorrect Sentence: There are many **softwares** available these days for various purposes.

Correct Sentence: There is a lot of **software** available these days for various purposes.

Incorrect Sentence: What does differrent between seems and seem?

Correct Sentence: What is the difference between seems and seem?

Incorrect Sentence: I am sorry, my computer have the problem.

Correct Sentence: I am sorry, there is a problem with my computer.

Incorrect Sentence: How is going everything?

Correct Sentence: How is everything going?

Incorrect Sentence: In fact I want my life had a little bit changed.

Correct Sentence: In fact I want to have some change in my life.

Incorrect Sentence: Oh, he has the same car with yours.

Correct Sentence: Oh, he has the same car like yours.

Incorrect Sentence: Joei, maybe I will sleepless after I saw his picture!

Correct Sentence: Joei, I may be sleepless tonight after seeing his picture!

Incorrect Sentence: He is trying to look cute to make himself forgiven.

Correct Sentence: He is trying to get away with it by looking cute.

Incorrect Sentence:	How do you think my idea?
Correct Sentence:	What do you think of my idea?
Incorrect Sentence:	Can you tell me when are you birthday date?
Correct Sentence:	Can you tell me when your birthday is?
Incorrect Sentence:	Could you correct me this letter?
Correct Sentence:	Would you correct this letter for me?
Incorrect Sentence:	John's work is more perfect than Tom's.
Correct Sentence:	John's work is better than/superior to Tom's.
Incorrect Sentence:	I am the only one graduated from high school.
Correct Sentence:	I am the only one graduating from high school.
Incorrect Sentence:	He has the aptitude for languages.
Correct Sentence:	He has an aptitude for language.
Incorrect Sentence:	I'm so much pleasing to talk with you.
Correct Sentence:	I'm so pleased/happy to talk with you.
Incorrect Sentence:	I'm very sorry for yesterday, but my chief returned and I must to leave the chatroom at once.
Correct Sentence:	I am sorry for my abrupt exit yesterday because my boss suddenly turned up.
Incorrect Sentence:	The discussion will begin after the dinner.
Correct Sentence:	The discussion will begin after dinner.
Incorrect Sentence:	Susan is incapable to complete the task by herself.
Correct Sentence:	Susan is incapable of completing the task by herself.

Incorrect Sentence: We make the bread with the flour.

Correct Sentence: We make bread with flour.

Incorrect Sentence: They study in the England.

Correct Sentence: They study in England.

Incorrect Sentence: Are they supported by Taliban or Iran?

Correct Sentence: Are they supported by the Taliban or Iran?

Incorrect Sentence: More and more people today die of the cancer.

Correct Sentence: More and more people today die of cancer.

Incorrect Sentence: I'll date her out this Saturday.

Correct Sentence: I'll take her out on a date this Saturday.

Incorrect Sentence: I like to play the football.

Correct Sentence: I like to play football.

Incorrect Sentence: Why don't stay more time here?

Correct Sentence: Why don't you stay a little longer?

Incorrect Sentence: The dogs are faithful animals.

Correct Sentence: Dogs are faithful animals.

Incorrect Sentence: The hunter took aim and then he shot the boar.

Correct Sentence: The hunter took aim and then shot the boar.

Incorrect Sentence: She has not answered to his question.

Correct Sentence: She has not answered his question.

Incorrect Sentence: We had a meeting in this afternoon.

Correct Sentence: We had a meeting this afternoon.

Incorrect Sentence: We better don't tell anothers.

Correct Sentence: We had better not tell others.

Incorrect Sentence: The experience is the best teacher.

Correct Sentence: Experience is the best teacher.

Incorrect Sentence: I bought a story book to read it.

Correct Sentence: I bought a story book to read.

Incorrect Sentence: Although he was ill, but he went to work as usual.

Correct Sentence: Although he was ill, he went to work as usual.

Incorrect Sentence: OK, I will see you late!

Correct Sentence: OK, I will see you later!

Incorrect Sentence: He is a more nicer person than you.

Correct Sentence: He is a nicer person than you.

Incorrect Sentence: I don't have enough money to buy big house.

Correct Sentence: I don't have enough money to buy a big house.

Incorrect Sentence: Am I complete right?

Correct Sentence: Am I completely right?

Incorrect Sentence: Why do you need hundred dollars?

Correct Sentence: Why do you need a hundred dollars?

Incorrect Sentence: I hate my boss, I feel like kicking on his butt.

Correct Sentence: I hate my boss, I feel like kicking his butt.

Incorrect Sentence: Japanese are industrious and frugal.

Correct Sentence: The Japanese are industrious and frugal.

Incorrect Sentence:	All these three cities are similar warm as Malaysia.
Correct Sentence:	All three of these cities are as warm as Malaysia.
Incorrect Sentence:	Will she come to there soon?
Correct Sentence:	She will go there soon, won't she?
Incorrect Sentence:	I seldom go to theatre.
Correct Sentence:	I seldom go to the theatre.
Incorrect Sentence:	Thanks, I no longer need to wait for anyone else's opinion anymore.
Correct Sentence:	Thanks, I no longer need to wait for anyone else's opinion.
Incorrect Sentence:	Smiths invited me to a dinner.
Correct Sentence:	The Smiths invited me to a dinner.
Incorrect Sentence:	Only I and my friend were at the concert.
Correct Sentence:	Only my friend and I were at the concert.
Incorrect Sentence:	Do you want to try my new car?
Correct Sentence:	Do you want to try out my new car?
Incorrect Sentence:	It is everybody's duty to defend their country.
Correct Sentence:	It is everybody's duty to defend his country.
Incorrect Sentence:	Many people in the past died from malaria.
Correct Sentence:	Many people in the past died of malaria.

Incorrect Sentence:	There are not anything wrong.
Correct Sentence:	There is nothing wrong.
Incorrect Sentence:	What is the time on your watch?
Correct Sentence:	What is the time by your watch?
Incorrect Sentence:	Kelvin, don't be so jealousy!
Correct Sentence:	Kelvin, don't be so jealous!
Incorrect Sentence:	Lucy has been absent from Monday?
Correct Sentence:	Lucy has been absent since Monday?
Incorrect Sentence:	The answer of this question is quite complicated.
Correct Sentence:	The answer to this question is quite complicated.
Incorrect Sentence:	Nobody is bound to suffering.
Correct Sentence:	Nobody is bound to suffer.
Incorrect Sentence:	The sales of light arms is the main cause of heavy casualty in conflicting nations.
Correct Sentence:	The sale of light arms to conflicting nations is the main cause of heavy causalities.
Incorrect Sentence:	Some people are not used to live in a hot country.
Correct Sentence:	Some people are not used to living in a hot country.
Incorrect Sentence:	Ah Ling, What is Hong Kong interesting?
Correct Sentence:	Ah Ling, What is in Hong Kong interesting?
Incorrect Sentence:	Nobody can avoid to make mistakes.
Correct Sentence:	Nobody can avoid making mistakes.

Incorrect Sentence: The judge has decided the case.

Correct Sentence: The judge has decided upon the case.

Incorrect Sentence: The students were busy to prepare their lessons.

Correct Sentence: The students were busy preparing their lessons.

Incorrect Sentence: I don't understand the meaning what you say.

Correct Sentence: I don't understand the meaning of what you said.

Incorrect Sentence: Please tell him don't come now.

Correct Sentence: Please tell him not to come now.

Incorrect Sentence: He took his girlfriend in the hand.

Correct Sentence: He took his girlfriend by the hand.

Incorrect Sentence: You had better to go now.

Correct Sentence: You had better go now.

Incorrect Sentence: The country is belonged to every citizen.

Correct Sentence: The country belongs to every citizen.

Incorrect Sentence: Mary felt sorry about the matter but she did not voice.

Correct Sentence: Mary felt sorry about the matter but she did not voice it.

Incorrect Sentence: Mary pretended to not recognize me.

Correct Sentence: Mary pretended not to recognize me.

Incorrect Sentence: Chen, you are informed. Thanks for your information.

Correct Sentence: Chen, you are informative. Thanks for your information.

Incorrect Sentence:	She neither speaks English nor Malay.
Correct Sentence:	She speaks neither English nor Malay.
Incorrect Sentence:	There is a dirty mark on the rug which must be removed.
Correct Sentence:	On the rug, there is a dirty mark which must be removed.
Incorrect Sentence:	Lizzie approached me and held my hand, said, "Hello !"
Correct Sentence:	Lizzie approached me, held my hand, and said, "Hello!"
Incorrect Sentence:	Is there some topic talk about?
Correct Sentence:	Is there any topic to talk about?
Incorrect Sentence:	Last one typhoon let person 4 hundred million damage.
Correct Sentence:	The latest typhoon has cost the people 400 million damage.
Incorrect Sentence:	Can the communism coexist with the capitalism?
Correct Sentence:	Can communism coexist with capitalism?
Incorrect Sentence:	I am worry about your English level will getting worse if you talk to me only.
Correct Sentence:	I am worried that your English will get worse if you only talk to me.
Incorrect Sentence:	David has just been commissioned as the captain.
Correct Sentence:	David has just been commissioned as captain.
Incorrect Sentence:	I saw them to work.
Correct Sentence:	I saw them work.

Incorrect Sentence: Am I a simple girl and has not any brains?

Correct Sentence: Am I a naive lady who doesn't have intelligence?

Incorrect Sentence: Just now my connection have problem.

Correct Sentence: I just had a connection problem.

Incorrect Sentence: This book is the most unique of all.

Correct Sentence: This book is unique.

Incorrect Sentence: Room's his windows are open.

Correct Sentence: The windows of his room are open.

at the eleventh hour: at the last minute; almost too late.

Example: Ratna finished it **at the eleventh hour**, but she wasn't late.

B

bad-mouth: say unkind, unflattering, embarrassing (and probably untrue) things about someone.

Example:

A: I don't believe what Bobby said! Why is he **bad-mouthing** me?

B: He's probably jealous of your success.

~~~~~~~~

be a piece of cake: be very easy.

Example:

Rita said the test was difficult, but Tina thought it was **a piece of cake**.

~~~~~~~~

be all ears: be eager to hear what someone has to say.

Example:

A: I just got an e-mail message from our old friend Shelly.

B: Tell me what she said. **I'm all ears**!

~~~~~~~~

be broke: be without money.

Example: Varun had refused to help as he **was** completely **broke** till payday.

~~~~~~~~

be in and out: be at and away from a place during a particular time.

Example: Could we postpone our meeting until tomorrow? I expect to **be in and out** of the office most of the day today.

~~~~~~~~

be on the go: be very busy (going from one thing or project to another).

Example: "I'm really tired. I've **been on the go** all week long," she said.

~~~~~~~~

be on the road: be traveling.

Example: "You won't be able to contact me tomorrow because I'll **be on the road,**" informed Tarun.

~~~~~~~~

be over: be finished; end.

Example: I can't see you until around 4 o'clock. My meetings won't **be over** until then.

~~~~~~~~

be up and running: (for a technological process) be operational; be ready to use

Example: Rohit Cafe on the Web has **been up and running** since December 2005.

~~~~~~~~

be used to: be accustomed to; not uncomfortable with.

Example: It won't be hard to get up at 5:00 a.m. **I'm used to** getting up early.

~~~~~~~~

beat: exhausted; very tired (adj.).

Example: This has been a long day. I'm **beat**!

~~~~~~~~
~~~~~~~~

beat around the bush: avoid an issue; avoid giving a direct answer.

Example: Quit **beating around the bush**! If you don't want to go with me, just tell me!

~~~~~~~~

beat one's brains out: try very hard to understand or do something.

Example: Can you help me with this problem? I've been **beating my brains out** with it, but I just can't solve it.

~~~~~~~~

beats me: I have no idea.

Example:

A: What time's the party?

B: **Beats me**!

~~~~~~~~

before long: soon.

Example:

A: I'm really tired of working.

B: Just be patient. The weekend will be here **before long.**

~~~~~~~~

bent out of shape: needlessly worried about something.

Example: I know you're worried about your job interview, but don't get **bent out of shape**. You'll do just fine.

~~~~~~~~

bite off more than one can chew: take responsibility for more than one can manage.
~~~~~~~~

Example: I'm really behind with my project. Can you help me? I'm afraid I **bit off more than I could chew**!

~~~~~~~~

blabbermouth: a very talkative person — especially one who says things that should be kept secret.

Example: Don't say anything to Mohan unless you want the whole office to know. Mohan's quite a **blabbermouth**.

~~~~~~~~

blow one's top: become extremely angry.

Example:

A: Was your father upset when you came home at 3 a.m?

B: He was more than upset. He **blew his top**!

~~~~~~~~

boom box: portable cassette/CD player.

Example: Don't forget to bring your **boom box** to the picnic!

~~~~~~~~

the bottom line: the most essential information.

Example: The discussion lasted many hours. **The bottom line** was that the ABC Company isn't for sale.

~~~~~~~~

Break a leg!: Good luck!

Example: I understand you have a job interview tomorrow. **Break a leg**!

~~~~~~~~

break someone's heart: make someone feel very disappointed/discouraged/sad.

Example: Nitin **broke his mother's heart** when he dropped out of school.

~~~~~~~~

C

call it a day: stop work for the day.

Example: It's late and you've accomplished a lot. Why don't you **call it a day**?

~~~~~~~~

can't make heads or tails of something: can't understand something at all; find something confusing and illogical.

Example: I **can't make heads or tails of** your e-mail. Were you having problems with your computer?

~~~~~~~~

catch one's eye: attract one's attention/interest.

Example: This brochure about Tripti **caught my eye** when I was at the travel agency.

~~~~~~~~

catch some Zs: sleep for a while; take a nap.

Example: You look tired, Dave. Why don't you **catch some Zs**?

~~~~~~~~

change one's mind: decide to do something different from what had been decided earlier.

Example:

A: Why are you working this week? I thought you were going to be on vacation.

B: I **changed my mind**. I'm taking my vacation next month.

~~~~~~~~

chow: food.

Example: How's the **chow** in the university cafeteria?

~~~~~~~~

chow down: eat.

Example: It's almost 6:00 p.m. Are you ready to **chow down**?

~~~~~~~~

a cinch: something that's very easy to do.

Example:

A: How was the test?

B: It was **a cinch**. I finished it quickly and I know that all my answers were correct.

~~~~~~~~

Cool it!: calm down.

Example: There's no need to be so upset. Just **cool it**!

~~~~~~~~

cost (someone) an arm and a leg: cost a lot; be very expensive.

Example:

A: Your new car is really nice.

B: It should be. It **cost (me) an arm and a leg**!

~~~~~~~~

couch potato: someone who spends too much time watching TV.

Example: You're a real **couch potato**, Jay. You need to get more exercise!

~~~~~~~~

cram: try to learn as much as possible in a very short time.

Example:

Sandy did well on the test because he **crammed** for it. However, he probably won't remember any of the information a couple of days from now.

~~~~~~~~

crash course: short course designed to give a lot of knowledge/ information in a very short time.

Example: Tony's company is sending him to a business meeting in Istanbul. Should he take a **crash course** in Turkish?

~~~~~~~~

D

Don't count your chickens until (before) they hatch (they've hatched): Don't assume that something will happen until it *has* happened.

Example:

A: I'm sure that I'm going to win a lot of money in Las Vegas.

B: **Don't count your chickens until they hatch!**

~~~~~~~~

dicey: uncertain; taking too much of a chance.

Example:

A: A friend of mine says I can make a lot of money if I buy stock in RST. Should I do it?

B: I wouldn't if I were you. The chances for success are too **dicey**.

~~~~~~~~

ditch class: skip class/play hookey.

Example: You shouldn't have **ditched class** yesterday. We had an unannounced test.

~~~~~~~~

do a bang-up job: do a very good job; do very well at something.

Example: Have you seen Farah's home page? She **did a bang-up job** with it.

~~~~~~~~

down in the dumps: depressed; blue.

Example:

A: Is something wrong?

B: Not really, but I feel kind of **down in the dumps**.

~~~~~~~~

drop someone a line: write to someone.

Example: I haven't written to my parents for a long time. I'd better **drop them a line** today or tomorrow.

~~~~~~~~

drag one's feet: delay; take longer than necessary to do something.

Example: Jatin should have finished his project a week ago. Why is he **dragging his feet**?

E

an eager beaver: a person who is always willing to volunteer or do extra work.

Example: Nikita is certainly **an eager beaver**. Whenever there's work to be done, she's the first to say she'll help.

~~~~~~~~
~~~~~~~~

Easy does it!: Be very careful! Don't do anything too fast or too hard!

Example:

A: I'm going to move the table just a little further from the window.

B: **Easy does it**! If you move too fast, you might knock over the plant!

~~~~~~~~

an egghead: a very intelligent person.

Example: Joy didn't make very good grades in school, but his sister was a real **egghead.**

~~~~~~~~

elbow grease: hard work; effort.

Example: Yes, the car is pretty dirty, but it'll look nice again with a little **elbow grease**.

~~~~~~~~

every other ____ : alternately; omitting the second one in each group of two.

Example: In your essays, please write on **every other line**. That will make the essays much easier to read.

F

far-fetched: difficult to accept; difficult to believe.

Example: That story's pretty **far-fetched**. Nobody's going to believe it.

~~~~~~~~

feel blue: feel sad and depressed.

Example: I'm **feeling blue** because I haven't had any mail except bills for a long, long time.

~~~~~~~~

fire someone: dismiss someone from a job because of poor performance.

Example: If you continue to be late for work, the company will **fire you**.

~~~~~~~~

feel puny: feel unwell, ill.

Example: Dad was **feeling puny** yesterday, so he decided not to go to work.

~~~~~~~~

for ages: for a very long time.

Example: Where's Marie? I haven't seen her **for ages**.

G

get going: leave.

Example: Look at the time! I'd better **get going**!

~~~~~~~~

get it: understand something (often negative).

Example: I don't **get it**. What do you mean?

~~~~~~~~

get a kick out of something: find something amusing.

Example: I really **get a kick out of** listening to children talk. They say some very funny things.

~~~~~~~~

get lost!: go away

Example: I wish he'd **get lost** and stop bothering me. I don't want to talk to him!

~~~~~~~~

get on one's nerves: irritate someone; make someone upset.

Example: I know you like that song, but it's **getting on my nerves**. Can you play something else?

~~~~~~~~

get a move on: hurry

Example: If you don't want to be late, you'd better **get a move on.**

~~~~~~~~

get one's wires crossed: be confused or mistaken about something.

Example:

A: Marie said there was a meeting this morning. Don't we have one?

B: No. The meeting's tomorrow. I guess Kanwal **got his wires crossed.**

~~~~~~~~

get out of hand: become out of control; become badly managed.

Example: Your absences are **getting out of hand**, Tina. You'd better do something quickly to improve the situation if you want to keep your job.

~~~~~~~~

Get real!: Be realistic!
~~~~~~~~

Example:

A: I'm going to Sydney. I know I'll win a lot of money!

B: **Get real!** You'll probably lose a lot of money!

~~~~~~~~

get up and go: energy.

Example: I'm really tired. I don't have any **get up and go**.

~~~~~~~~

give someone a hand: help someone.

Example: I can't do this alone. Can you **give me a hand**?

~~~~~~~~

a (real) go-getter: a (very) ambitious, hard-working person.

Example: I'm not surprised that Kiran finished before anyone else. She's **a real go-getter**.

~~~~~~~~

go with the flow: take things as they come.

Example: There's no need to worry. Everything will be OK if you just **go with the flow**.

~~~~~~~~

grab a bite: get something to eat.

Example: I'm really hungry. Would you like to **grab a bite** with me?

~~~~~~~~

green: inexperienced.

Example: I don't think you can depend on Joy to do that job by himself. He's too **green**.

H

had ('d) better: be obliged to; should (strong).

Example: You'**d better** leave soon. If you don't, you'll miss your bus.

~~~~~~~~

hassle (noun): a troublesome situation; something troublesome that interrupts one's normal routine.

Example: I know it's **a hassle** to complete this form now, but Mr. Roman needs it in his office by the end of the day.

~~~~~~~~

hard feelings: anger; animosity; bitter feelings.

Example:

A: I'm sorry that Raghu got the job instead of you.

B: I have no **hard feelings** toward him; I know that he had more experience.

~~~~~~~~

hard-headed: stubborn; inflexible; unwilling to change.

Example: I don't think Juliet will change her mind. She's pretty **hard-headed**.

~~~~~~~~

have one's hands full: be extremely busy.

Example:

A: Will you be able to help us this afternoon?

B: I'm afraid not. I'll **have my hands full** trying to finish my research paper.

~~~~~~~~
~~~~~~~~

have something down pat: know/understand something completely and thoroughly.

Example: I know I did well on the test. I **had** all the material **down pat**.

~~~~~~~~

hit the books: study.

Example: I wish I could go to the movies, but I've got to **hit the books**.

~~~~~~~~

hit the hay: go to bed; go to sleep.

Example: It's late, so I guess I'll **hit the hay**.

~~~~~~~~

hit the sack: go to bed.

Example: I'm really tired. I think I'll **hit the sack**.

~~~~~~~~

How come?: Why? (Statement word order).

Example: **How come** you weren't at the party?

I

if I had my druthers: if I could do what I wanted/preferred.

Example: **If I had my druthers**, I'd stay home from work today.

~~~~~~~~

in over one's head: in a situation that is too much / too difficult for one to manage.

Example: Do you have time to help me? I thought I could do this myself, but I'm afraid I'm **in over my head**. I just can't handle things alone.

~~~~~~~~

inside out: with the inner part on the outside and the outer part on the inside.

Example: Why are you wearing your tee shirt **inside out**?

~~~~~~~~

in stock: in supply and available to buy / sell.

Example: I'm sorry, but we just sold our last pair of hiking boots. If you come back at the end of the week, however, we should have some more **in stock**.

~~~~~~~~

in the black: profitable; not showing a financial loss.

Example: What did you do to increase profit and eliminate losses? We've been **in the black** for two months in a row.

~~~~~~~~

in the red: unprofitable; showing a financial loss.

Example: We have to do something to increase profit and decrease losses. We've been **in the red** for two months in a row.

~~~~~~~~

in time: not late.

Example: I thought I was going to be late for my flight, but it was delayed, so I was still **in time**.

J

jump all over someone: severely criticize / find fault with someone.

Example:

A: What's wrong with Abhinav?

B: He's feeling bad because his boss **jumped all over him** this morning.

~~~~~~~~

jump the gun: do something before it's time to do it.

Example:

A: How did Rohan know about the party? It was supposed to be a surprise.

B: Nitin **jumped the gun**. Without thinking, he said, 'I'm bringing the cake at your party; I hope you like it!

~~~~~~~~

jump to conclusions: decide something too quickly and without thinking about it or considering all the facts.

Example:

A: Angel just doesn't like me. She won't even say hello.

B: You're **jumping to conclusions**. Actually, she's very shy.

~~~~~~~~

junk mail: unsolicited mail (usually advertisements for something you're not interested in).

Example: I didn't have any letters today — only **junk mail**.

K

keep an eye on: check something regularly.

Example: You're busy, so you'll need to **keep an eye on** the time. Remember that we have to leave at 4:30.

~~~~~~~~

keep an eye out for: watch for.

Example: I'll **keep an eye out for** Naveen. If I see him, I'll tell him you want to talk to him.

~~~~~~~~
~~~~~~~~

keep one's chin up: remain brave and confident in a difficult situation; don't despair or worry too much.

Example: I know that things have been difficult for you recently, but **keep your chin up**. Everything will be better soon.

~~~~~~~~

keep one's nose to the grindstone: stay diligent; steadily work hard, without breaks or an uneven pace.

Example: If I **keep my nose to the grindstone**, I should be finished by the end of the day.

~~~~~~~~

keep/stay in touch (with someone): remain informed (about someone) / in contact (with someone) by writing, calling, sending e-mail, etc. on a regular basis.

Example: I haven't seen Mohan for two or three years but we **keep** (stay) **in touch** by e-mail.

~~~~~~~~

keep one's fingers crossed: hope for the best.

Example:

A: How did you do on the test?

B: I think I passed, but I won't know until tomorrow. I'm **keeping my fingers crossed**!

~~~~~~~~

kid (noun): child.

Example:

A: You have three **kids**, don't you?

B: That's right. I have two girls and a boy.

~~~~~~~~
~~~~~~~~

kid (verb): playfully say something that isn't true.

Example: I was **kidding** when I said my teacher was a monster. She's strict, but she's actually a very nice person.

~~~~~~~~

kind of: rather; more or less; a little.

Example: I'm feeling **kind of** hungry. I think I'll make myself a sandwich.

~~~~~~~~

a know-it-all: someone who acts as if he/she knows everything — as if no one can tell him/her anything that he/she doesn't already know.

Example: Don't try to make any suggestions to Bharat. He's **a know-it-all** and won't pay attention to anything you say.

~~~~~~~~

know something backwards and forwards: know/understand something completely and thoroughly.

Example: If you have a question about HTML tags, ask Suman. She **knows** HTML **backwards and forwards**.

~~~~~~~~

know something inside out: know/understand something thoroughly.

Example: If you have a question about grammar, ask Dr. Mittal. She **knows** grammar **inside out**.

L

lend someone a hand: help someone.

Example: I can't do this alone. Can you **lend me a hand**?

~~~~~~~~
~~~~~~~~

leave well enough alone: do nothing (because doing something would make things worse).

Example: Don't tell Jimmy how to discipline his children. **Leave well enough alone**.

~~~~~~~~

a let-down: a disappointment; something that's very disappointing.

Example: It must've been quite a **let-down** not to be chosen for that job. I know you really hoped you would get it.

~~~~~~~~

let sleeping dogs lie: Don't cause problems by doing something when it isn't necessary.

Example: I know that what Rita said made you angry, but **let sleeping dogs lie**. If you say or do anything, you'll only make things worse.

~~~~~~~~

live from hand to mouth: survive on very little money; have only enough money to pay for basic needs.

Example: Kavita is **living from hand to mouth** since she lost her job.

~~~~~~~~

live and let live: don't unnecessarily make things difficult; do as you wish and let others do as they wish.

Example: I'm not going to criticize Alice's family just because their habits are a little strange. My motto is '**Live and let live**.'

~~~~~~~~

a low blow: a big disappointment.
~~~~~~~~

Example:

A: Sidharth seems depressed. Is he OK?

B: He's OK, but not good. It was **a low blow** for him to be laid off from his job.

~~~~~~~~

lousy: terrible; very bad.

Example: Why did you speak so rudely to your grandmother? That was a **lousy** thing to do!

M

macho: super masculine / masculine to an extreme (in appearance and behaviour).

Example: Her husband would never agree to help with the housework; he's too **macho** to do that.

~~~~~~~~

make a mountain out of a molehill: make something seem much more important than it really is.

Example: Calm down. There's really nothing to worry about. You're **making a mountain out of a molehill.**

~~~~~~~~

make up one's mind: decide what to do.

Example:

A: Where are you going on your vacation?

B: Maybe Canada, maybe Mexico. I can't **make up my mind**.

N

No way!: Absolutely not! / definitely not!
~~~~~~~~

Example:

A: You didn't open this letter addressed to me, did you?

B: **No way**! I'd *never* look at some else's mail!

~~~~~~~~

nosh: snack.

Example: There's plenty in the refrigerator if you want something to **nosh** on.

~~~~~~~~

Not on your life!: Absolutely not! (a strong no).

Example:

A: Someone said you cheated on the test. Did you?

B: **Not on your life**!

~~~~~~~~

now and then: occasionally; from time to time.

Example:

A: Do you see Jennifer often?

B: No, not really. I see her **now and then**, but not regularly.

~~~~~~~~

nuke: heat in a microwave.

Example: If your coffee's cold, just **nuke** it for about a minute.

~~~~~~~~

nuts: crazy.

Example:

A: Stuart says some really strange things sometimes.

B: Sometimes? All the time! He's **nuts**!
~~~~~~~~

O

OK: (1) yes (to show agreement—often reluctant agreement).

Example:

A: Come on, Fardeen. We really need your help!

B: Oh, **OK**; I may be crazy, but I'll help you.

~~~~~~~~

OK: (2) neither good nor bad; so-so.

Example:

A: How was the movie?

B: **OK**, I guess, but I've seen better ones.

~~~~~~~~

OK: (3) in satisfactory condition; well.

Example:

A: You look awfully pale. Are you **OK**?

B: Actually, I'm not. I have a terrible headache.

~~~~~~~~

OK: (4) approve (verb).

Example:

A: Did your boss **OK** your vacation plans?

B: No, but he said that taking them two weeks later would be all right.

~~~~~~~~

on the dot: exactly at a given time.

Example: We're leaving at 9:00 **on the dot**. If you're late, we'll go without you.

~~~~~~~~
~~~~~~~~

on time: at the scheduled time.

Example: It's getting late. You'd better hurry if you want to get to work **on time**.

~~~~~~~~

(on the) cutting edge: using the most recent technology.

Example: The university's computer lab is **(on the) cutting edge**. It has all the latest hardware and software.

~~~~~~~~

once in a while: occasionally; from time to time.

Example:

A: Would you like coffee or tea?

B: Coffee, please. I drink tea **once in a while**, but I generally drink coffee.

~~~~~~~~

P

pay the piper: face the consequences for something you've done.

Example: I stayed up too late tonight. Tomorrow I'll have to **pay the piper**.

~~~~~~~~

plastic: credit card(s).

Example: Oh, no! I forgot to get any cash! I hope this restaurant accepts **plastic**!

~~~~~~~~

pooped: very tired; exhausted.

Example: I went to bed really early last night. I was **pooped**!

~~~~~~~~

pop quiz: unannounced short test.

Example: You shouldn't have missed class yesterday. We had a **pop quiz.**

~~~~~~~~

pretty (adv.): rather; somewhat.

Example: That car's **pretty** expensive. Are you sure you can afford it?

~~~~~~~~

pull an all-nighter: study or work all night without getting any sleep.

Example:

A: You look really tired.

B: I am. I **pulled an all-nighter** to get ready for the meeting this morning.

~~~~~~~~

pull someone's leg: tease someone by trying to make her/him believe something that's exaggerated or untrue.

Example:

A: Wow! Kavita has done some really amazing things!

B: Don't believe everything she tells you. She was probably **pulling your leg.**

Q

quite a few: several; numerous.

Example: I don't think I can meet you after work. I have **quite a few** errands that I have to do.

~~~~~~~~

a quick study: someone who learns new things quickly and easily.

Example:

A: Anita seems to be doing well at her new job.

B: I'm not surprised. She's **a quick study**.

R

rain or shine: (describing something scheduled) no matter what the weather is.

Example: We're leaving tomorrow, **rain or shine**.

~~~~~~~~

rain cats and dogs: rain very hard.

Example: You can't leave just now! It's **raining cats and dogs.**

~~~~~~~~

read someone's mind: know what someone is thinking.

Example:

A: I know you're thinking of what you're going to have for dinner.

B: Hey, did you **read my mind**?

A: No. I just know that you're hungry and lunch was several hours ago!

~~~~~~~~

rub someone the wrong way: irritate someone; bother someone.

Example: All my little brother says is 'Why?' Usually I'm patient with him, but sometimes all his questions **rub me the wrong way**.

~~~~~~~~

run-down: (1) not well; weak; fatigued.

Example: Are you eating regularly and getting enough sleep? You look **run-down**.

~~~~~~~~

run-down: (2) in poor condition; needing repair.

Example: This must be a poor neighbourhood. All the buildings look really **run-down**.

S

-savvy: knowledgeable about something.

Example:

A: If you're having problems with your hard disk, talk to Rohit.

B: He's **computer-savvy**.

~~~~~~~~

shoot the breeze: make relaxed, casual conversation.

Example:

A: We weren't talking about anything important.

B: We were just **shooting the breeze**.

~~~~~~~~

sleep on it: take at least a day to think about something before making a decision.

Example: The job that you're offering me sounds really good, but I'd like to **sleep on it** before giving you my final decision.

~~~~~~~~

a snap: something that's very easy to do.

Example:

A: Is your job difficult?

B: No, actually it's **a snap**. In fact, it's so easy that it's a little bit boring.

~~~~~~~~

sooner or later: eventually.

Example: You've been working too hard for too long. If you don't relax a little, **sooner or later** you're going to get sick.

~~~~~~~~

sort of: rather; somewhat.

Example: I think I'll lie down. I feel **sort of** dizzy.

~~~~~~~~

state of the art: using the latest technology.

Example: The company is very proud of the equipment in its computer room. It's **state of the art**.

~~~~~~~~

Step on it!: Hurry up!

Example: **Step on it**! The taxi will be here at any time and you're not even dressed!

T

take it easy: relax.

Example: I don't have any special vacation plans. I'm just going to **take it easy**.

~~~~~~~~

tell a white lie: say something that isn't true in order not to hurt or offend someone.

Example: The cake that Suman made tasted terrible, but I knew that she made it because she wanted to please me, so
~~~~~~~~

when she asked if I liked it, I **told a white lie** and said it was good.

~~~~~~~~

tough: difficult.

Example: Question number three is a **tough** one. Do you know the answer?

~~~~~~~~

There, there.: expression of comfort.

Example: **There, there**. Everything's going to be OK.

~~~~~~~~

a tightwad: someone who is very frugal and unwilling to spend money unnecessarily.

Example:

A: Will Charlie donate any money to the activities fund?

B: Absolutely not! He's a real **tightwad**!

~~~~~~~~

tricky: easily confused or misunderstood.

Example: This problem is **tricky**. I don't really understand it.

~~~~~~~~

two-faced: deceitful; disloyal; someone who pretends to be a friend but isn't.

Example: I thought he was my friend, but he's **two-faced**. He says nice things to me when we're together, but makes jokes about me when we aren't.

U

under the weather: ill; sick; unwell.
~~~~~~~~

Example: Dad was feeling **under the weather** yesterday, so he decided not to go to work.

~~~~~~~~

until you're blue in the face: forever.

Example: You can talk **until you're blue in the face,** but I won't change my mind.

~~~~~~~~

update: make current; add information to show what has happened recently.

Example: I need to **update** my résumé. It doesn't show what I've done during the last year.

~~~~~~~~

upside down: with the bottom part on top and the top part on bottom.

Example: Put the glasses **upside down** in the dishwasher. If you don't do that, they'll fill with water and you'll have to dry them by hand.

~~~~~~~~

used to: an action that was true in the past but is not true now.

Example: Jane **used to** live in Australia but she lives in San Francisco now.

W

wear out one's welcome: make someone uncomfortable by visiting too long.

Example:

A: Can't you stay two or three more days?

B: No. I don't want to **wear out my welcome.**

~~~~~~~~
~~~~~~~~

What's up?: What's new? What's happening?

Example: Hi, Hemant! **What's up?**

~~~~~~~~

wishy-washy: uncommitted; without an opinion of one's own.

Example: Don't be so **wishy-washy**. Tell us how you really feel.

~~~~~~~~

with bells on: very eagerly; with the feeling that one will have a very good time.

Example:

A: Are you going to Sandra's party?

B: I'll be there **with bells on**!

Y

You don't say!: Really? / Is that really true?

Example:

A: Have you heard the news? Jessica got married!

B: **You don't say!**

~~~~~~~~

You've got to be kidding!: You can't be serious! (What you said can't be true. What you said is very surprising/hard to believe.)

Example:

A: Did you know that Bobby quit his job?

B: **You've got to be kidding**!

~~~~~~~~

yucky: terrible; distasteful; very unpleasant.

Example: Don't eat the soup at the cafeteria. It's **yucky**!

~~~~~~~~

yummy: delicious.

Have you tried those cookies? They're **yummy**!

Z

zilch: nothing.

Example:

A: How much money do you have?

B: **Zilch**. I'm broke until payday.

~~~~~~~~

Zip your lip!: keep something secret; promise not to tell what has just been said.

Example: What I told you is really important, so **zip your lip**!

■■■